CALL SIGN DRACULA

My Tour in Vietnam with the "Black Scarves"
April 1969 to March 1970

JOE FAIR

D1198294

SUNBURY
P R E S S

Mechanicsburg, Pennsylvania   USA

Published by Sunbury Press, Inc.
50 West Main Street, Suite A
Mechanicsburg, Pennsylvania 17055

www.sunburypress.com

For information about special discounts for bulk purchases, please contact Sunbury Press Orders Dept. at (855) 338-8359 or orders@sunburypress.com.

To request one of our authors for speaking engagements or book signings, please contact Sunbury Press Publicity Dept. at publicity@sunburypress.com.

ISBN: 978-1-62006-388-0 (Trade Paperback)
ISBN: 978-1-62006-389-7 (Mobipocket)
ISBN: 978-1-62006-390-3 (ePub)

FIRST SUNBURY PRESS EDITION: April 2014

Product of the United States of America
0 1 1 2 3 5 8 13 21 34 55

Set in Bookman Old Style
Designed by Lawrence Knorr
Cover by Lawrence Knorr
Edited by Amanda Shrawder

Continue the Enlightenment!

Author's Note

Images of the battles, events, tragedies, and deaths are forged in my mind forever. The dreams (sometimes nightmares) still come. Almost every day, even after all these years, a thought of Vietnam goes through my mind; it may bring a tear, a smile, or a question. I cannot just forget all that happened.

One must attempt to live in peace with oneself, rejoice in making it home alive, and having the honor to have served proudly with the best young men America had to offer: my fellow soldiers.

"About a soldier: Don't preach to him about losses, he knows the meaning of death."

Danger Forward,
(the magazine of the Big Red One),
Spring, 1970.

Acknowledgments

I must provide an acknowledgement and special thanks to my long-time friend, Wendell Rainwater. He took me to the airport when I left home heading to Vietnam and was there to pick me up when I came home, one year later. Wendell was the last person from home I said good-bye to and the first person from home to welcome me back.

I must recognize my loving wife, Regnia (Gina Gail) who has been by my side since July 18, 1970. She has been my strongest supporter, partner, and friend.

Many thanks to Diana and Patrick Keefe of Campbellsville, KY for the many hours they spent editing the book. My grammar, spelling and use of punctuation were very poor.

I also want to give many thanks to Lawrence (Larry) R. Grzywinski, the Historian for the 2nd Infantry Regiment Association, for his valuable input and information. He served with the HHC (Headquarters and Headquarters Company), 2nd Battalion, 2nd Infantry Regiment in Vietnam during 1966 and 1967. He is a "walking encyclopedia" when it comes to the 2nd Infantry Regiment's time in Vietnam. He has helped me tremendously in making the book as accurate as possible.

I must thank my children and their spouses: Brad and Natasha Wright, Mark and Jennifer Jones, and Derick and Jaime Fair. They listened to me as I constantly talked about Vietnam and the book. They encouraged me to continue writing.

I must say thank you to Jan and Steven Spruill. Jan was the sister of Joe Spruill, one of my best friends in Vietnam. She set the stage for Steven and I to make contact. Steven, a first cousin to Jan and Joe Spruill and a well-known author, believed in "Call Sign Dracula" from day one. He helped me tremendously and was most instrumental in making it all happen. I am forever in his debt and proud to call him my friend.

Last but not least, I am so thankful for all my family and many friends who were there for me when I left for Vietnam and were there for me when I returned. There are just far too many to attempt to name. Vietnam was a very negative war to many. When I came home, I was a hero to them. My family, friends and community were and remain today very patriotic.

Above all, I must thank God for everything.

Introduction

All the fine soldiers I had the opportunity to serve with made this account possible. They were my comrades and my friends. It is written from my perspective; how I saw Vietnam.

Notes

Unit Assignment:
Lima (1st) Platoon, Alpha Company, 1st Battalion, 2nd Infantry Regiment, 1st Infantry Division, US Army

About the division, regiment and battalion:

1st Infantry Division—The "Big Red One"
> Motto: "No Mission Too Difficult, No Sacrifice Too Great, Duty First." The Division fought in Vietnam from 1965 to 1970.

2nd Infantry Regiment-—"Ramrods"
> Motto: "Noli Me Tangere" (Do Not Touch Me) – the 3rd oldest regiment in the U S Army.

1st Battalion—The "Black Scarves"—(call sign Dracula)

1st Battalion 2nd Infantry Regiment – "Black Scarves"
> "On 30 April 1966 in a sweep through the village of Lo Go, the 1st Battalion was engaged in heavy fighting and it was during this time that a large quantity of black cloth was captured. This cloth was used by the Viet Cong to make their 'Black Pajama' uniforms. At the direction of battalion commander, Lieutenant Colonel Richard Prillaman, this cloth was made into scarves to be worn by the battalion's soldiers. Lieutenant Colonel Prillaman wanted to be able to distinguish his battalion from other division soldiers and to provide the soldiers with something

more appropriate than the towels the men were wearing around their necks. It is from this that the battalion has as its nickname 'Black Scarves.' The battalion call sign was changed from 'Docket' to 'Dracula' during this same time frame. The Battalion was being used for night operations and along with the wearing of the black scarf call sign "Dracula" was most appropriate. The printing on the scarves was a different color for each company: HHC= yellow, Company A= red, Company B=white, Company C= blue and Company D= green."

Area of Operation:
South Vietnam, III Corp, War Zone C & D

There is a probability of inaccuracy with dates, times and places as I am using mostly my memory and the memories of my fellow soldiers. The events did happen and are as factual as possible. I apologize for any errors found within this document. If there are any, none were intentional. If I have offended anyone in any way, I sincerely apologize.

A book from Vietnam, ***The 1ˢᵗ Battalion, 2ⁿᵈ Infantry, 1ˢᵗ Infantry, Dracula–1969***, was most valuable in helping me remember names of those I served with; it is a priceless book. I would like to offer a special thanks to my Vietnam Platoon Sergeant, Michael Schellenberger, for loaning me his book. I lost mine while still in Vietnam.

A special thanks to my fellow soldiers that I have been in contact with over the past year; it has been awesome talking with these guys. They have helped revitalize my memory and shared their stories. I hope I have not left anyone out:

Alex Sole - Pennsylvania
Roy Bohn - Texas
Thomas Coker (Captain) - Colorado
Dom Zazarro (Lieutenant) - Virginia
Dwayne Ellrich - Indiana
Roger LaSante - New Hampshire
Elmo Taylor (Doc) - Utah
Mike Hart (Lieutenant) - Minnesota
Bob Childers - Texas

Ron Hume - Texas
Roger Johnson - Minnesota
Berl Martin - Iowa
Steven Gray - Oregon
Cary Dawkins - North Carolina
Bob Faubert - California
Jerry Allen - North Carolina
Pete Elsos - Washington
Jeff Mill - Connecticut
Michael Schellenberger (Shelly) - Kentucky
Jim Ward - Ohio
James Marx (Butch) - Pennsylvania
Marty Vazanna - Michigan
Mike Sears - Florida
Monte George (Lieutenant) - Pennsylvania
Dale Rilling - South Dakota
Tom Drake – Michigan
Peter Bernardini- North Carolina

I must say thanks to my mother and father. They saved every letter I sent home. The letters were most instrumental in establishing places, dates, and events. When my father passed away in January 1988, my mother told me that he had insisted on saving each letter and piece of information that I sent home or that the US Army sent to them. My dad was very proud of me. He was a proud WWII veteran. I sure was proud of him and it was an honor to be his son and call him Dad.

Here are the cities, base camps and firebases I was at during my tour. I believe these are in the correct order of when I was there. We did bounce back and forth from some:

Tan Son Nhut Air Base, just a mile or so northwest of Saigon

Long Binh - 90th Replacement Battalion, just a mile or so northeast of Saigon

Di An - 1st Divisions' Support Command HQ, 5 miles north of Saigon

Lai Khe - 1st Divisions' HQ and Base Camp, 25 miles north of Saigon

Quan Loi Base Camp, 60 miles north of Saigon and just east of An Loc

Fire Support Base Song Be, 80 miles north of Saigon - this was the farthest north we operated

An Loc, 60 miles north of Saigon

Fire Support Base Thunder II, 10 miles south of An Loc right off Highway 13

Fire Support Base Pine Ridge sat on top a range of mountains we called the "Razor Backs." From here you could see for miles.

Dau Tieng Base Camp, 45 miles northwest of Saigon

Fire Support Base Mahone, 5-6 miles south of Dau Tieng

Notable landmarks and places:
Nui Ba Den - Black Virgin Mountain, the most notable landmark in III Corp.
Nui Ba Ra - Sister Mountain to the Black Virgin Mountain, FSB Song Be sat right next to this mountain.
Razor Backs - FSB Pine Ridge sat on top of this mountain range.
Michelin Rubber Plantation - a huge rubber plantation at Dau Tieng. It covered many, many square miles. The rubber trees were planted in almost perfect rows. It was very easy to navigate in and had many crisscrossing roads. At Dau Tieng, our Battalion Headquarters occupied one of the large French plantation homes.
The Iron Triangle – a dense jungle area south and south east of the Michelin Rubber Plantation that was a haven for the enemy.
The Ho Chi Minh Trail - a logistical system of roads and trails that ran from the Democratic Republic of Vietnam (North Vietnam) to the Republic of Vietnam (South Vietnam) through the neighboring kingdoms of Laos and Cambodia. The system provided support, in the form of manpower and material, to the National Front for the Liberation of South Vietnam (called the Vietcong or "VC") and the

People's Army of Vietnam, or North Vietnamese Army (NVA), during the Vietnam War.

The 1st Battalion's Headquarters was at Lai Khe when I joined the unit. While at Lai Khe the unit also worked out of Quan Loi, Song Be, Thunder II and An Loc. In June, the Headquarters was moved to Dau Tieng. From there, the unit also worked out of FSB Mahone and FSB Pine Ridge.

First Infantry Division's Area of Operation

Chapter One

April 1969

I arrived in Vietnam the very early part of April 1969 at Tan Son Nhut Air Force Base that was a mile or so northwest of Saigon. I was a PFC (Private First Class).

PFC Phillip Warren, my hometown friend, and I were together in Infantry Advanced Individual Training (AIT) at Ft. Polk, LA. We flew to Vietnam together. It was good having someone you knew at a time like that.

I remember flying in on a military commercial flight on Braniff Airways. When I first spotted Vietnam from the air, I thought how beautiful and green it was. When the airplane touched down I muttered to myself, "Well, here I go. I have twelve months to go and I've just started."

I was hoping I would get in with some real good guys. In the back of my mind, I was hoping to be assigned to the 1st Infantry Division—the "Big Red One." I had seen a Vietnam Veteran at Fort Polk who was an instructor. He wore the "Big Red One" patch. He was a good instructor and spoke well of the 1st Infantry Division. I thought I'd like to get into that unit.

I looked at Phillip and asked, "Are you ready for this?"

He just nodded his head, somewhere between a yes and no. I could see doubt in his eyes. Perhaps he saw the same in mine.

When I walked off the plane and the hot, humid air hit me, I thought, *my gosh, it sure is hot. This is going to be rough.* It was 95 degrees with super high humidity. I had just left the US in late March. In Kentucky, it was 35-40 degrees.

Tan Son Nhut was a large Air Base. I saw a lot of planes and fighter aircraft that really amazed me. I noted in the air a lot of helicopters. I soon learned that you could hear and see aircraft (mainly helicopters) in the air virtually 24 hours a day.

1

JOE FAIR

There I was in my brand new jungle fatigues, baseball cap, boots and carrying my duffel bag. I stood six feet one-and-a-half inches and weighed in at 150 pounds. I knew that I looked brand new. As we were lining up to board a bus, there were other troops who were leaving Vietnam. They were lining up to board a plane. Some were shouting at us, "Hey look at the 'cherries' (new guys). Now aren't they cute!"

Some were set on giving us a hard time as they were laughing and joking about us being their replacements. Some of them just gave us the thumbs up and a nod of the head. I noted some just looked down and never looked at us. Their uniforms were well worn and they were all deeply tanned.

I was impressed. These guys had just completed a year tour. They were veterans: combat soldiers. I wanted to be one of them.

From the Air Base, we moved by bus to Long Binh. I wondered how many soldiers before me had gone through this same process and travel. Riding through the city and then the suburbs, I was amazed at the Vietnamese people. All the bicycles, motorcycles, mopeds, and the three wheel passenger mopeds that I learned later we called Lambrettas. Some of the women were wearing pants outfits with some kind of split dress over it. Later, I learned the outfits were called "Ao Dai." I saw lots and lots of black silk pants and white shirts and blouses. Black pants and white shirts/blouses were the dominant clothing and colors. It seemed that everyone was wearing sandals, and there were lots of large hats that looked like straw hats. I saw some Vietnamese soldiers wearing sidearms. This was a new world for me.

I kept thinking, as we rode the bus, *we haven't been issued our weapons and here we are in a combat zone.* What would we do if we got hit? I noticed the bus driver, who was an army soldier, was not armed. He didn't seem to have a worry in the world. It just seemed strange to me and I was really concerned.

At Long Binh, I went into the 90th Replacement Battalion to await assignment to my unit. As we unloaded the bus, we turned in our field jackets and some gear that we were told we didn't need. I recall having to stand in a line with a bunch of other new troops and brush my teeth with special, chlorinated toothpaste for about 30 minutes. This was to help fight tooth decay, since we were in a war zone where maintaining proper dental hygiene posed a problem. The sergeant kept telling us to brush, brush, brush.

That night, my first night in Vietnam, I was assigned guard duty at Long Binh in a bunker on the base perimeter with a young black fellow. We had an M60 machine gun, tons of ammunition and two M16 rifles that we had to turn back into the armorer the next morning. I wanted to keep mine.

The front of our bunker was well lit, with rows and rows of concertina wire. We had to report via a TA 312 field phone every 30 minutes that all was well. It was 2 hours on, 2 hours off. The young black guy and I were scared to death. We kept talking about what to do if we were attacked. I had the right field of fire and he had the left. We would, over and over again, check the M60 to make sure it was ready to fire. We kept checking our M16's to make sure they were loaded. The next morning, I said good-bye to the young black guy and wished him well. I never saw him again. (Later in my tour, I found out that Long Binh was one of the safest places to be in all of Vietnam. Of course, we didn't know it our first night in country).

My next day at Long Binh, as I was going through the chow line, PFC Crowder, whom I had been with at Fort Polk during AIT (Advanced Individual Training), hollered out at me. It was good seeing him. He was on Kitchen Police (KP). We only talked briefly, just a minute or two, as he was behind a screened window washing food trays. We said good-bye and wished each other the best. That was the last I saw of him.

He was a good friend at Fort Polk, which was where we were trained to be infantrymen with an 11B MOS (Military Occupational Specialty). Troops called it an Eleven Bravo MOS. I do not know what became of him. He is not listed on the KIA (Killed in Action) list of Vietnam. He had written Mom and Dad asking for my address. I still have the letter.

My second night, I was assigned guard duty at a swimming pool. Now that impressed me. I didn't even have a weapon. Officers were having a pool party with lots of food and beer. When the party was over, I looked at the raw steaks on the barbecue, the baked potatoes, salad and beer. I figured, "what the hell," and grilled myself a steak. I really enjoyed the food and beer.

The Sergeant of the Guard was making his rounds and observed me eating and having a beer. I remember him asking, "Private Fair, what the hell are you doing?"

I informed him that I was soon going to the bush and the steaks and beer were going to waste. What were they going to do to me? You have to make the best of every situation. That's what I was trained to do.

He shook his head, smiled and moved on. That was the first time I ever had a grilled steak.

The next day, I checked the duty assignments and was surprised to find I was assigned to the 1st Infantry Division. The 1st Infantry Division's AO (Area of Operation) was north and northwest of Saigon. I got what I wished for. When I was talking to some other troops about assignments, they wished me good luck as the "Big Red One" was a tough unit and known to be hardcore. They were right, but it was a damn good unit with a great history.

I recall my Dad telling me that I wasn't too smart after I told him about the written screening we took at the US Army Reception Center at Ft. Knox, KY. Part of the screening asked if I liked the outdoors, was I sure footed, and did I like shooting? I told my Dad I had answered yes to these questions. He said, "Hell son, you just volunteered for the infantry."

Well, there I was, assigned to an infantry unit. Dad was right of course.

Phillip Warren saw from the assignment list that he was going to the 82nd Airborne. The 82nd Airborne's AO was south and southwest of Saigon. Phillip and I said our good-byes, shook hands, wished each other the best and departed.

It was sad watching him walk away. *I sure hope we both make it through the next year and go home all in one piece.* That was the last I saw or heard from Phillip until I got home in March 1970. He had also made it home unscathed.

Phillip passed away in early 2013. Seeing him lying there in a coffin sure brought back memories of our time together training at Fort Polk, LA and our short time together in Vietnam. He was my friend and a good soldier.

From Long Binh, the 1st Infantry Division's replacements were bussed to Di An. Di An was the 1st Infantry Division's Support Command Headquarters. We were assigned to the 1st Infantry Division's Replacement Detachment while we waited for our unit assignment. At Headquarters there was a very large, concrete Big Red One. It really stood out and caught the eye. It must have been 20 feet high. Posted on a sign at the base of this large statue was the divisions' motto: "No Mission Too Difficult, No Sacrifice Too Great, Duty First."

The Sergeant who met us told us to remember the motto and we had better know our chain of command. Well, I knew President Nixon was the President and Commander-in-Chief, Melvin Laird was the Secretary of Defense and Stanley Resor was the Secretary of the Army. These had been drummed into our brains at Ft. Knox, KY and Ft. Polk, LA. But here I didn't have a clue as to the rest of the chain of command. I had just gotten here. When I joined my Company I would figure it all out. That same day, I did note on a sign that Major General Orwin Talbott was the 1st Infantry Division Commander. I made a mental note of that.

My first day at Di An, I was put on sh-t burning detail. That just goes with the life of a Private. You pulled the cut-in-half 55 gallon drums from the latrines, poured diesel fuel in the drum, lighted the fuel, watched as the human waste burned, and stirred the mess to make sure all waste was burned. What a great detail.

As I was going on this detail, I climbed into the back of a deuce-and-a-half (2.5 ton truck) where there was a young black soldier sitting there. He was in a new uniform just like me and was also a Private. We started talking and of course he asked where I was from. I told him Kentucky and he asked what part. I told him Campbellsville and he informed me that was where he was from. Go figure—travel

8,000 miles from home, be amongst 600,000 troops and bump into a guy from your hometown. Wow, did we enjoy our time together that day. His name was Ernie Johnson. I didn't know Ernie, but we knew lots of the same people.

A real funny thing happened as I was pulling one of the drums from the latrine; an old Vietnamese woman was using it. As I pulled the drum out, she started hollering, of course in Vietnamese, and we didn't understand a word she said. I quickly shoved the drum back in. Finally, she came out of the latrine and looked at Ernie and me and was jabbering loudly and pointing her finger at us. She was pulling her pants up tying them in place. All we could do was smile. Later on, we learned that "boo koo dinky dau," meant we were really crazy.

Ernie was in communications and was assigned to the 121st Signal Battalion. When we departed, Ernie told me to "take care, and best of luck." I had told him I was an infantryman. He told me I needed some extra good luck. That was the last time I saw Ernie until I went to work for Ingersoll Rand in September 1971. Ernie was working there. Man, it was sure good to see him again. We told the employees about our time together in Vietnam and burning sh-t. It was a big hit. Ernie still holds a special place in my heart.

At Di An, we were issued our M16 rifles and ammunition. Finally, I had my weapon! We went through remedial training; patrolling, setting up an ambush, loading onto and off mocked-up UH1 helicopters. *More training, and we are doing it in a combat zone*, I thought. We also trained on using C4 explosives and detonation cord. That was new.

The 1st Infantry Division had a long and proud history dating back to World War I. We were given a brochure: *Welcome to the Big Red One*. I read it and found it quite interesting. It told about the history of the Division, our Area of Operation in Vietnam and about who the enemy was. I also read where Major General Keith Ware, the 1st Infantry Division Commander was killed in September 1968. I thought the enemy must have been proud of that. For some reason, I didn't think a General would get that close to the fighting. I was wrong. Later, I learned there were several General Officers killed in Vietnam. I still have the brochure after all these years. It is one of many of my small treasures from Vietnam.

From Di An, we moved to Lai Khe, Headquarters for the 1st Infantry Division, via a convoy on Highway 13. Lai Khe was nicknamed "Rocket City." It was known for all the indirect fire pounding (rockets and mortars) it took from the enemy. The Battalion Headquarters was also at Lai Khe at this time.

On the back of a deuce-and-a-half (2.5 ton truck) I was assigned with a black guy named Gunn. He was a Private and a "Cherry" like me. We had our M16's and also an M60 machine gun. Gunn was a talker and it didn't take me long to figure him out. I could tell he would be a troublemaker and I needed to stay clear of him. He had a gold plated front tooth that had what looked like a spade formed in it. I thought, *how strange*. It is amazing to me how little things such as that gold tooth can remain in one's mind so well. Later, we were assigned to the same Company and it didn't take long for him to get in real trouble and sent to LBJ (Long Binh Jail). I don't know what happened, but rumor had it that he pointed a loaded pistol at one of our officers.

I vividly recall riding in the deuce-and-a-half behind the M60 machine gun that had sand bags piled around it to form a fighting position on the back of the truck. I kept a sharp eye on the jungle and rubber plantation as we went through both. I just knew we were going to be ambushed; we were sitting ducks. Luckily, we made the trip with no difficulties.

At the Battalion Headquarters, I read the sign and learned that Lieutenant Colonel Thomas Rehm was the Battalion Commander. I never met him. I was taken by a ¼ ton (jeep) from the Battalion Headquarters to the Company area.

The first guy I met in the unit was Staff Sergeant Palmquist. He was the NCO (Non-commissioned Officer) in charge of the Rear Operations. He was a super nice guy and really tried to help me. He had done his time in the jungle and was an experienced combat soldier. I sure looked up to him and wondered what all he had seen and done. Sitting on his desk was a human skull. I assumed it was a VC (Viet Cong) or NVA (North Vietnamese Regular Army) soldiers' skull. I thought it was probably a war trophy. I never heard the story behind it. That skull stayed with Alpha Company my entire tour. It is in several photos.

There I elected to have all my monthly pay sent home except for $20 per month. I wanted Mom and Dad to have the money. The military recommended keeping $75 per month. I thought that was way too much. After three months I had $60. I didn't spend a dime. When I did get home, Mom and Dad had saved every penny I sent. My Mom and Dad were my heroes.

The money we used in Vietnam was called Military Payment Certificate or MPC. There were no coins. It was all paper (Nickel-Dime-Quarter-Half Dollar, then Dollar, Five Dollar, Ten Dollar, Twenty Dollar). You could have a billfold full of paper money and not have much. The MPC was not to be used by the Vietnamese people, unless they were under work contract by the US, but of course they did use it.

Every now and then, without advanced notice, the military decided to change the MPC. Soldiers would exchange their current MPC with the new MPC. This caused havoc with the Vietnamese, as they would have a lot of MPC but no way to exchange it for the new issued MPC. Old Mama San (old woman) and Papa San (old man) would get stuck with a lot of MPC that was worthless. It seemed unfair, but that was the rule.

The military was not supposed to use Vietnamese money, which was called piasters or dong. I didn't use or have any. It was against the law to have or use US currency in Vietnam. As soon as you arrived in country, you exchanged your dollars for MPC. I managed to bring home with me a ten-cent piece of MPC. I may have broken the law. I still have it today.

I was issued a Vietnam Military PX Ration Card. The best I can recall the card was pale orange and white, would fold out and had two sections. The card was used when you were at the PX buying beer, liquor and cigarettes. This was on section one. Section two was for items such as a watch, camera, projector, tape recorder, electric fan, typewriter, record player and refrigerator. You were allowed to purchase so much cigarettes, beer and liquor per month. The other items you could only purchase so many or even one in your entire one-year tour. I was told the restrictions were due to the black market. GI's would buy the items and sell them to the local Vietnamese for a huge profit. I used the card maybe one or two times my entire tour. We didn't get to go to the PX that often, and what the thunder was I going to do with an electric fan or refrigerator?

I spent the night in Lai Khe and was quartered in a semi-permanent building, which had a metal roof and wooden sides with screens. Cots were provided so it was fairly comfortable. I just knew I needed to enjoy this little luxury while I could. Staff Sergeant Palmquist told me to locate the closest bunker to move to just in case we started receiving in-coming rounds. That directive sure made me stop and think. I knew I was getting closer and closer to the enemy.

I was flown by helicopter from Lai Khe to Quan Loi to join my unit the next morning. This was my first ride in a helicopter and I had many, many more rides to come. When I arrived, the unit was still in the bush. I met William Wright, Forward Supply, who issued more equipment to me. He was a good guy and had done his time in the bush.

That afternoon, after getting my issue of a rucksack, canteens, poncho, poncho liner, ammunition, rations, water, etc., and a black scarf, I flew out to the jungle with the resupply chopper and joined my unit. I was the only replacement on the chopper. I got off the chopper and a soldier took me to the Company CP (Command Post). I met Captain Scully, the Company Commander, and First Sergeant Miller, the senior NCO (non-commissioned officer) in the Company. I was told Captain Scully was a graduate of the Army's West Point Military Academy. The First Sergeant, or "Top," as he was sometimes called, was an older man who had been in the Army for quite some time. He was what we called a "Lifer" or a career soldier. I still recall he was very tall, big and bald. They welcomed me to the unit and told me to pay attention to my Platoon Leader,

Platoon Sergeant, Squad Leader and the others in my Squad.

They didn't have to tell me that. I knew I needed to watch and listen.

The soldier then took me to 1st (Lima) Platoon and I was introduced to the Platoon Leader Lieutenant Domenic Zazarro from New Jersey, and Platoon Sergeant Dale Rilling from South Dakota. Both were really nice, helpful and welcomed me to the unit. I was then assigned to my Squad and introduced to Spec-4 Rock (Mike) Davis from Minnesota, Spec-4 Ernest Cartwright, Spec-4 Earnest Freeman from North Carolina, and Private First Class David Demings from Oklahoma. Unfortunately, I don't recall where Earnest Cartwright was from. They helped me get my stuff organized (it was called getting your sh-t together) so that I could carry it in the jungle.

Davis and Freeman told me to get rid of my T-shirt and underwear, as I wouldn't need them. Wearing underwear was a bad idea due to heavy body perspiration, causing skin rash and jock itch. So I stripped off right there and trashed my T-shirt and drawers. I was given a starlight scope (night vision scope or "Green Eye," as it was called by the troops) to carry. It was in a carrying case and was quite heavy and cumbersome. Every soldier carried something special: M60 ammo, grenades, smoke grenades, etc. I was told to carry a green towel with me. Later on, I discovered how important it was. The green towel was used as a sweat rag, pillow, padding for your shoulder, and of course a drying towel. I was told to wrap my billfold in plastic to keep it dry. Freeman gave me some plastic that was wrapped around the new PRC 25 radio batteries that came with the resupply.

So there I was in the jungle with steel pot (helmet), M16 rifle, rucksack, 3 quarts of water, 2 quart bladder bag of water, first aid pouch, ammo pouch with 20 magazines, Claymore mine with detonator, 6 C-ration meals, poncho and liner, a dry pair of socks, foot powder, bug repellent, 2 smoke grenades, 2 hand grenades, a block of C-4 explosive, bayonet, starlight scope (night vision scope), entrenching tool, green towel, black scarf, and writing paper. And that's why they called us "Grunts." Every step we took we made a grunt.

Freeman told me to make sure I only loaded eighteen rounds in each of my M16 magazines. The magazine was made for twenty-rounds, but the troops had learned that if fully loaded the spring in the magazine had a tendency to jam. He also showed me how to tap the magazine on the side of my steel pot (helmet) just before I placed the magazine in the M16. This helped align the rounds within the magazine and prevented jamming.

I found out that when we were patrolling in the bush we called it "humping." I was instructed to wrap black or green tape around the handle of the hand grenades (the troops called them frags). This was an additional safety measure to keep the handle in place, just in case the pin got caught and pulled out by the heavy vegetation we walked through. It made sense, and I didn't ask any questions.

I remember quite well moving out on my first real patrol and thinking there was a gook (slang for our enemy) behind every tree. I was a "cherry" and quite scared. I was definitely on high alert. My senses were super keen. Then it rained, and I got cold from being wet. There was no place to escape to in order to get out of the rain. There was only talking in whispers. No loud noises. Hand signals were used to tell everyone to stop, hold in place, move forward or get down. My equipment and rifle were heavy, and I could really feel the effects. The walking and carrying the stuff was kicking my butt real good. The harness straps were rubbing my shoulders. My steel pot was heavy and killing my neck. My boots were eating at my feet and blisters were starting to form. If I wasn't cold from the rain, I was hot from the scalding sun and humidity I kept thinking: *how do these guys do it?*

"Hang in there," Demings would tell me. "You'll soon adjust."

He'd only been with the unit about four to five weeks, but already he was quite tough.

Luckily for me, we were picked up by choppers three days later and flown back to Quan Loi for two days of rest. I don't know if I could have made another day. Those guys took me under their wings and really tried to take care of me, being a new guy to the unit and bush. When we talked about things, I was a "newbie." I had less time "in country" than the other guys. I listened more than I talked. Rock Davis told me to do my job, do it well and don't try to be a hero. He said, "We all watch out for each other."

I just knew I could depend on these guys if the going got rough.

Our showers were just a wooden structure with a tin roof. Large drums were placed on top of the structure. The drums held the shower water. Most of our showers were with cold water, but every now and then we would get hot water. There were gasoline fired submersible heaters they placed in the drums, which heated the water. A hot water shower was an absolute luxury. Soap was provided by our supply, but shampoo was another luxury item.

At the firebases and base camps we also had what we called the "pisser." This was a 55-gallon drum buried three-fourths of the way into the ground. It was filled with rocks and had a metal screen over the opening. Here is where male soldiers urinated. Some did have a three-sided wooden partition for some privacy. We had little, if any, privacy. That was the life of a soldier in a combat zone.

The army had two types of water: potable and non-potable. Potable was for drinking and cooking. Non-potable was for washing, showering and washing clothes, but was not safe for drinking.

Our Areas of Operation were all called free fire zones. That meant permission was not required prior to firing on the enemy. The guys told me to fire it up and not to hesitate if we made contact. I could not imagine operating in enemy territory where you had to get permission prior to firing on targets. There were some areas in Vietnam that had such restrictions. It just didn't make sense to me. I always assumed it was to help prevent killing innocent Vietnamese civilians. Years later, I was appalled at how many Vietnamese were killed during the war. It is mind-boggling.

Chapter Two

May 1969

At Quan Loi, the dirt was red and it seemed to get into everything. When it rained, it became red mud that stuck to everything. Even today when I talk to soldiers who had been at Quan Loi, they recall the red dirt. Quan Loi was also occupied by units of the 1st Cavalry Division (Airmobile) and the 11th Armored Cavalry Regiment (Blackhorse). Both were darn good units and were well respected by everyone.

I got to ride on a "mule" at Quan Loi. The 1st Cavalry unit used them extensively. It was a small, gas-powered, 4-wheel vehicle. It was a flat wooden bed sitting on four wheels with a steering wheel. It reminded me of the hand-powered carts used by the railroad to move up and down the tracks. I had seen some of these in old western movies. The official nomenclature of the mule was M274 truck, platform. I had bummed a ride while walking to the small PX (Post Exchange). The 1st Cavalry guys were great. I remember the driver asking me how much time I had left.

"Over 300 days," I told him.

He just smiled and told me he had less than 100 days. He was a "Two-Digit Midget" (less than 100 days left in country). "What part of the world are you from?" He asked. The troops called the United States "The World."

I told him Kentucky, and he said, "That's cool man. Kentucky's a good place. You have all that bluegrass and all that gold stored there."

I believe he told me he was from California. He dropped me off at the PX and told me to take care. I wondered what all he had seen and done during his tour, and I wondered what lay ahead of me.

I soon found out that all the troops tracked their days left in country. It was a big deal and provided a goal to work toward.

I never saw that driver again.

It was there that one of the lieutenants (who wore glasses and was really fair- skinned) was practicing judo or some form of Karate with some type of pointed daggers in each hand. He seemed to know what he was doing and did it quite well. I watched him dance, move and swing for quite some time. *How strange,* I thought, but I guess it was his way of dealing with being in Vietnam. Later, I learned that it was Lieutenant Monte George from Pennsylvania, an Artillery Forward Observer assigned to our Company. Lieutenant Zazarro told me this past year that Lieutenant Monte George was an excellent Forward Observer who could accurately and rapidly call artillery fire and direct air support onto targets. He was one of the best.

At the firebases and base camps, a jeep or ¾ ton truck was rigged to spray clouds of insecticide through the exhaust system to help with mosquitos. Usually right after dark, the cloud of insecticide would be sprayed all around the base. It would choke you somewhat if you were caught in the cloud, but it sure helped with getting rid of those darn aggravating pests.

Ronald Gray from Illinois and Marty Vazanna from Michigan, were swapping tales about the last few days in the bush. These two were in the weapons squad (4th Squad). Ronald Gray was a big talker and I really liked him. Marty was much more quiet and I really liked him also.

These guys are experienced and have seen a lot, I thought. *I need to listen to and follow them.*

I overheard them talking about two of their friends, PFC Milford Looney from Alabama, and Sergeant Willie Malone from Texas, who were killed on March 16, 1969; these two guys had been killed by mortar rounds fired into the Platoon position. I could tell they were still very upset over the deaths of Looney and Malone.

Freeman, Cartwright and I went to see a movie they were showing at Quan Loi. I remember it was a vampire movie, but it was also a comedy. If my memory is correct, Gene Wilder was one of the stars. The movie was shown outside on a white sheet. The seats were homemade wooden benches. There wasn't any popcorn and candy. I recall walking with Freeman and Cartwright to and from the movies. Both were tall and lanky. Cartwright was quite skinny and had a real funny gait to his walk. Freeman was just a good old country boy from Morganton, North Carolina. Both were just good guys who cared about others. We became friends.

I felt very close to Freeman (Earnest was his first name) as we were both hillbillies and we kind of talked the same. I could tell he liked me. He told me he had joined the unit in late October 1968 and that he had an "Old Lady." Sometimes the guys used the expression "I have an Old Lady," when they told you they were married.

We pulled guard duty at our assigned bunker along the perimeter at Quan Loi. The entire perimeter was well lit with huge lights on poles. There were rolls and rolls of concertina wire. Chain link fence, Claymore mines and trip flares were placed in front of each bunker.

I experienced my first "Mad Minute." A "Mad Minute" was a concentrated fire of all weapons for a brief period of time at maximum rate; also called "Mike-Mike." We fired our M16's and the M60 machine gun. Wow, seeing every bunker along the entire perimeter firing all their weapons was a sight to see. It was impressive.

The guys were teaching me how to tell out-going rounds versus in-coming rounds. The Artillery and Mortar sections were virtually firing non-stop. If you heard a thump then a whistle, screech or wop-wop-wop, it was in-coming. That is when you would hear everyone shouting, "in-coming!" and scrambling for cover. We would dive into bunkers and just pile right on top of each other. You could see almost every soldier pause and listen every time a round was fired to determine if it was in-coming or out-going. It was a way of life.

I noted on the left side of our shirts under the pocket was the 2nd Infantry Regiment's logo. It had written in Latin the words "Noli Me Tangere." It may have been Latin, but it was "Greek" to me. Of course, I asked some of the guys what that meant. I was told it translated to "Not Me Turkey." I gathered from some of the looks the guys were giving each other that this was a big joke. I even think I saw a wink or two. It took another week or so for me to learn that it meant, "Do Not Touch Me."

The guys also explained to me about the idea and history of the black scarf we wore and the battalion call sign "Dracula." I was proud to be one of the "Black Scarves." You could readily pick us out from all the rest of the troops in Vietnam, as we proudly wore our black scarves around our necks. Each company of the "Black Scarves" had a specific color to signify their company. Alpha Company was red. I still have a black scarf today. It is priceless.

Nearly every night in the bush we "dug in." That meant we used our entrenching tool and dug a fighting position, or—as the old timers called it—a "foxhole." It was most important to have at least a berm or mound of dirt piled up in front of you so that if you started receiving fire you could get behind it. The digging was quite easy as the soil was very sandy and loose. During the monsoon, or rainy season, the hole would fill up rapidly with rainwater. But still, it was a hole to get into if you started receiving fire. Under fire, that water in the hole didn't mean a thing.

We were air lifted by chopper from the firebases or base camps to LZ's (Landing Zones) in the jungle. We were also picked up from PZ's (Pick-up Zones) and taken to the firebases or base camps. The LZ's were just open areas that allowed the choppers to land. Most of the time, but not all the time, the LZ's were pounded with artillery or mortar rounds prior to our arrival. We called this prepping the LZ. This helped to ensure the LZ's were safe to land in. A HOT LZ was where we were landing under fire. That was not a good situation. Troops never liked to land in a LZ that wasn't prepped. Sometimes we could move out from the firebase and walk directly to the jungle. This didn't happen very often. Our main mode of transportation was the chopper. We made so many combat assaults via the choppers that we were all awarded air medals. I received an air medal and two oak leaf clusters. Each oak leaf cluster meant another award. So, I had three.

I recall the choppers flew around 1500 to 2000 feet to avoid the range of an AK47 (the main weapon of our enemy). I recall as we approached the LZ, the choppers would dive down from the 1500 to 2000 feet level to tree top level that allowed an unobserved approach to the LZ. Some of the chopper rides were wild and exciting

A couple of times we were flying and had to hit the deck (drop from the 1500 to 2000 feet level to tree top level) as all of a sudden an emergency artillery mission was being fired. You had to immediately drop lower than the artillery rounds being fired or face the risk of being hit in the air. Wow, it was a ride to drop so suddenly! We all hung on and prayed we wouldn't get hit by an artillery round or crash into the jungle or open areas with such a rapid descent. We were always concerned about receiving ground fire. Dying in a crashing, burning chopper was a great concern for all.

Rivers and streams were blue lines on the military maps, so that is what we called them in the bush. If we came to a river or stream, while patrolling, we would call back that we were at a blue line.

We moved out again from Quan Loi. Patrolling and setting up ambushes was always our mission. We patrolled every day and virtually every night an ambush was set up.

Demings and Freeman showed me how to use a small piece of C4 (an explosive) to heat C-rations (this was against regulations). Using expensive C4 to heat rations was an absolute no-no, but soldiers soon learn how to take advantage of every situation. Once lit, never attempt to extinguish the C4 by stomping it out. You could blow your foot off!

I learned that we called the small can opener used to open the C-ration cans a P38. Troops would stick the small can opener in the elastic band around the steel pot. We always saved our empty cans that held fruit to make coffee. I liked coffee in the morning and they told me never to use the apricot can for my coffee water. The apricots always left a bad taste.

I soon learned what the best C-rations were and most favored. Beans and franks, ham slices, and turkey slices were the most favored. Ham and lima beans and then ham and eggs were the worst meals you could get. Even the Vietnamese knew how bad the ham and eggs were. They were number ten, which meant "not good" to the

Vietnamese. You could get by on beef and potatoes and meatballs and spaghetti. There was also a meal we called LRRP (Long Range Recon Patrol) rations. They were excellent, but we didn't get very many. Hot sauce was a constant staple for the C-rations.

I learned about the candy bars in the C-rations the guys called "John Wayne" bars. They were edible, but really not good. I was taught how to place the small chocolate paddy that came in some C-rations between two crackers to make a really good snack. It doesn't sound good, but it really was. It was a good energy boost.

Peanut butter, called "choke" by the troops, came in a small can. Along with crackers, it was a good snack. I wrote home and my Mother sent me packages of instant oatmeal. That's what I had just about every morning in the bush.

Bless Paula, my sister, and my Mom and Dad for they sent me a package every three to four weeks. A special note: When I got home from Vietnam, Roy Wethington, our Postmaster, told me about Paula, Mom and Dad coming to the post office at least twice per month and mailing me a package. They were very dedicated to making sure I got things. I love them dearly.

Our ambushes were typically along a trail or road and sometimes along a route designated as an easy travel area. Many of the trails and roads were part of the Ho Chi Minh Trail system. Our ambushes were squad (7-10 men) or platoon (25-35 men) size. We would establish 3-4 men fighting positions about 15-20 meters from the kill zone of the ambush. Claymore mines were set along the kill zone. We would establish firing lanes into the kill zone from each fighting position to ensure we had full coverage of the kill zone for our M16 rifles and our M60 machine guns. Then we watched and waited.

When we blew an ambush the Claymore mines were detonated, the M16 rifles and M60 machine guns were fired. We saturated the kill zone with intense fire. If we blew an ambush at night we would pull back from the ambush sight to a rally point that was typically 20-30 meters to the rear and wait until dawn to check the kill zone. If we blew the ambush during the day we would check it out immediately after the firing ceased. During my time in the bush, we blew many ambushes that resulted in several kills. Our ambushes were effective. Our kill numbers were very good. It was a form of grading. The units with a high kill number were considered the better units.

When we killed an enemy soldier, we would sometimes tie one of our black scarfs around his neck and just leave him lying where he was killed. We wanted the gooks to know they had tangled with the 1st Battalion 2nd Infantry ("Black Scarves, Call Sign Dracula"). I was told the gooks had a bounty on our heads. I never heard how much. I think this may have been just hype talk trying to make us feel good and convince others that we were a bunch of mean asses.

I walked as point man (lead man on a patrol) and slack man (directly behind the point man). I got rid of that darn starlight scope. It was customary for the new guys to walk point. This had my pucker factor very high at first, but soon I became more accustomed to it. I kept telling myself that it was like squirrel hunting, like I had done many times at home, except these squirrels fired back.

We just had to stay focused and look and listen intently. We moved slowly and with as little noise as possible. The point Squad Leader would point in the direction we were to travel. I was fortunate while walking point I didn't come upon any gooks or lead the unit into an ambush.

It was almost impossible to walk in a straight line in the thick jungle. One guy in the Platoon or Squad kept track of how far we had gone by counting paces and estimating our travel in meters. We called 1,000 meters a "klick." A grid square on our maps was 1,000 meters by 1,000 meters. The Squad Leaders, Platoon Sergeant, Platoon Leader, and Company Commander would all have a compass and map and kept us on course and in the right area. Getting lost could be a disaster. Our leaders were well trained and darn good.

We came upon a gook bunker complex. I believe it was Davis who spotted it first and alerted us. It was well hidden and looked to be about a platoon size area with about 10-

12 bunkers. We must have surprised them, as the fire pits still had hot embers, and they had left some of their equipment. We found sandals, pants, shirts, food, and an older Russian SKS bolt-action rifle. Rice and fish was their main staple. We found two bags of rice. No automatic weapons or RPG (rocket propelled grenades) were found. The bunkers were well built with overhead cover. We were extremely careful and made sure there were no booby-traps. The area was called into Headquarters. We destroyed the bunkers and moved out.

I tried different methods to carry my stuff. I used the butt pack and put C-ration cans in socks and tied them to the butt pack. The butt pack just wouldn't accommodate all my stuff and had a tendency to slap me in the butt with every step. That didn't work so I went back to the rucksack, which was by far the best.

Boy, could the body really smell bad after days in the jungle. Soon we all smelled the same and we didn't notice. We did practice hygiene as best we could in the bush. We brushed our teeth, washed our hands, combed our hair and washed our body when time and circumstances allowed.

I found out that to help stay awake on guard duty all you had to do was pull your shirt up over your nose and get a shot of your own body odor. The body odor was like a shot of ammonia. Every night in the bush each soldier pulled two to three hours of guard in their position. To fall asleep while on guard was a cardinal sin. Typically we got 4-5 hours of sleep each night in the jungle. We would catch short catnaps during the day when we stopped for a rest period or to chow down. Someone in each position was always on guard.

We started working with the 11th ACR (Armored Cavalry Regiment) whose base camp was also at Quan Loi. They were mechanized so we got to ride on M113 APC's (armored personnel carriers). The 11th was an incredible unit—a real bunch of good guys and they were wild. I remember some had names painted on their track vehicles. The one that stuck in my mind was: Hard, Horny and Helpless. In my mind, I still clearly see that track vehicle and the guys even after all these years.

We made contact with the enemy outside Quan Loi. I remember jumping off the M113 and getting behind it for protection. The M113 had an M2 .50 caliber machine gun and two M60 machine guns, so they were really laying the fire down. As we advanced forward, firing our weapons, I saw a dead gook lying beside a tree. My first look at the enemy and he was dead. He was in full khaki uniform, and I knew he was an NVA (North Vietnamese Regular Army). There were some green tracer rounds coming back toward us, but none close to our APC. When a round is fired at you there is a loud crack as the bullet passes, then you hear the sound of the weapon firing. These are two distinct sounds: crack, then pop. I was so scared that my heart was pounding and I was shaking. We just kept firing and moving forward. I didn't see the enemy, but fired my M16 along with all the others.

Finally, after what seemed like an eternity, but was just a few hours, the firing stopped. We established a NDP (night defensive position) and remained in place overnight. We dug in beside the tracks. Sitting in a position with the APC's made me feel like we presented a big target for an RPG (rocket propelled grenade). The APC crew placed chain link fence around the front about two feet from the track vehicle. This helped stop an RPG round. The round would detonate when it hit the fence and not hit the vehicle. The sky was cloudy and it was pitch black.

I helped set trip flares in front of our positions. These were set at the most likely approach the enemy would take to get to our positions. Trip flares were early warning devices. They were well camouflaged and had a very small trip wire that went from the flare across a path or an approach and tied to a bush. The idea was the enemy would walk into the trip wire and set off the flare and alert us. The trip flare produced a brilliant white light and really lit up the area. They were an excellent part of our defense.

The next day we were patrolling again with the mechanized unit. I remember Jim Wheeler of Ohio, our M79 grenade launcher man, jumping off the M113 and hitting the ground hard. One of the crew on the M113 thought he saw movement and started firing his M60. Wow, how fast Wheeler moved. It was kind of funny seeing

Wheeler move so fast and hard. Several of us gave him a helping hand to get back on board. He was smiling and we were laughing. He took it well. Small things like this made life in a combat zone more bearable.

We moved to FSB Song Be. The firebase sat right next to a mountain that was called Nui Ba Ra. I was told it was the sister mountain to Nui Ba Den, the Black Virgin Mountain. At Song Be, the Company went outside the perimeter one day and we practiced firing our weapons. We all got in line and were told to commence firing. I assumed Captain Scully thought we needed it. Lieutenant Zazarro was there and directing us where to fire. We were firing into a trash dump. To me, and many of the troops, it seemed like a waste. We fired a lot of rounds then had to clean our weapons. If there was a benefit to this I couldn't figure it out.

I was adjusting to the jungle and the heavy equipment, so I started carrying ammo for the M60. I was moved to 4th Squad. It was the weapons squad. Marty Vazanna was an M60 Gunner in 4th Squad. Now that really kicked my butt every day: two cans of M60 ammo (each can had 100 rounds of 7.62 machine gun ammo). The pure weight of the ammo and drudging through the jungle was an hourly challenge. There were days that I focused on just putting one foot in front of the other to make it. But soon I became more adjusted and physically more capable of carrying the heavy load and bearing the difficulties of the jungle. The ammo cans were also good storage for writing paper and letters from home. They slid right in with the ammo.

One day we commenced a long, long march that Captain Scully was leading. We were told we were attempting to intercept a large NVA force that was on the move in the Michelin Rubber Plantation. We walked for hours and hours and the troops were really feeling the effects. I was so tired I couldn't even think right. I remember Captain Scully grabbing my ammo cans and we marched on. What a relief it was for me for the short time he carried those damn cans.

We walked well into the night and we all kept thinking this couldn't be good. Captain Scully kept telling us to march on. Finally, we stopped and started setting up our

NDP (night defensive position). We dug in as best we could. I remember very well setting up our Claymore mines. After we placed the mines along a likely approach we moved back to our fighting positions.

Remember, now it's dark, and almost pitch black.

All of a sudden one of the Claymores went off!

A troop had accidentally hit his detonator. It scared the hell out of everyone. Luckily no one was hurt. We didn't sleep much that night even though we were totally exhausted. We all felt the gooks knew exactly where we were. Why we made such a move in the dead of night is beyond me. It just didn't make tactical sense.

Each day I was getting more acclimated to the jungle, the heavy gear, and realizing the enemy was not behind every tree. I was listening to the guys who had been there for quite some time and learning from them. The older, more experienced guys were sharp and darn good at patrolling, recognizing where and when the enemy had been in the area, picking ambush sites, alerting us to slow down or get down, and knowing where we were at all times. They instructed us on setting up the ambushes that included where to place the M60 machine guns, Claymore mines and how to cut fields of fire for our M16's. They showed us the hand signals we were to use. They knew where we were on the maps, how to call in artillery fire support, request MEDEVAC (choppers to pick up wounded, sick or injured soldiers), and how to make radio reports using coded messages. The radio was called the "horn." They would check our weapons, gear, make sure we had water and rations, and kept us informed of what our mission was and if it changed. They looked out for every individual soldier. They were the best, incredible leaders, and I would readily follow them into hell and back. They were that good and by gosh they were tough. I knew I needed to be like them. When I say "older," I mean more time in Vietnam, in the jungle.

We were *all* so young.

I had the pleasure of hugging a really good-looking Donut Dolly at Song Be. I have the photo. Wow, was she good looking! There were two or three that were flown in by helicopter to the fire support base. They were there to boost our morale. Well, it worked for me. My wife always asks me to explain every time she sees this photo.

I soon learned that none of us knew what day of the week it was. It really didn't matter anyway. We had a 24 hour per day, seven day per week life. If someone asked what day of the week it was, it was a strange feeling not knowing. We knew what month and calendar date it was as our operations depended on the date. Sunday through Saturday didn't mean a thing to us.

We got used to whispering in the bush. So much so that when we came out of the bush to a more secure place we all found ourselves still whispering. The rear troops thought we were crazy. Habits tend to stay with you.

On May 9, David Peterson from Minnesota, and Lieutenant Guy Pratt from Oklahoma were killed in a firefight outside of Quan Loi. I believe they were in Mike Platoon. The Company was in-line walking from an open area into the jungle. It was called a skirmish line. We were told there was a VC (Viet Cong) unit operating up in this area and it was believed they had a bunker complex in front of us.

We moved into the wood line and were attempting to encircle the suspected bunker complex. All of a sudden, our platoon could hear heavy firing coming from a good distance away to our front. The firing was intense for a short period of time. Then we received fire from our left, deep in the jungle, and we started firing and moving forward. The intelligence reports were correct, as we had a VC bunker complex to our left. I had moved up and fell to a prone position to the left side of Vazanna, the M60 Gunner. My head was close to the barrel as he fired. The loud noise was deafening and I had loud ringing in my ears, especially my right ear.

We established a defensive perimeter. We had not made the complete encirclement.

Word got to us that Lieutenant Pratt and Peterson had been hit and that MEDEVAC (also called a dust-off) was on the way. Dwayne Ellrich of Indiana held the hand of Lieutenant Pratt until he was placed on the helicopter. Dwayne and Lieutenant Pratt were very good friends. Later, we learned that Lieutenant Pratt died in the helicopter flying to the hospital at Quan Loi. We were told Peterson had been killed.

The fighting picked up again and was so intense we pulled back and left Peterson's body. We had several wounded soldiers including one of our medics, Peter Bernardini of North Carolina, who was wounded attempting to get to Peterson to render aid. Air strikes and Artillery were called in. The area was hit hard, both by bombs from the planes and rounds from the Artillery. You just can't imagine how everyone felt having to leave a comrade's body in the bush. Mike Platoon returned to the jungle the next day and recovered his body. Peterson had just returned to the unit from the 1st Infantry Division's Sniper School. It is sad, but I don't recall what Pratt or Peterson looked like. Just this past year, Butch Marx told me how devastating it was to find Peterson's body the next day and load him on a helicopter.

On May 10th, we were back at patrolling in the bush. I developed a large cyst on my right forearm and was running a high fever. It started out as just a small sore. I was shivering even in the heat of the jungle. The Medic checked me out and deemed that I needed immediate medical attention. We had to walk to an open area.

I recall how sick I was. I felt terrible.

Vazanna, Demings and Freeman helped carry my gear and weapon. MEDEVAC was called and I was air lifted out of the jungle to Delta Med at Quan Loi. This was my first and only ride in the small LOH (light observation helicopter). This chopper was in the air in our area and received the radio report to pick up a sick soldier. I climbed into the very small rear area behind the pilots' seats. It was a short ride to Quan Loi. At the hospital in Quan Loi the doctors examined me, then opened the cyst and allowed it to drain. I was given an antibiotic shot in the hip every 6 hours for my first 24 hours. I think they called it a staph infection. At the time, I didn't know what that meant. The hospital was set up in a metal building, but the recovery wards were tents.

There were several men in the same tent as me. Some were from the 1st Infantry Division, 1st Cavalry Division, 11th Armored Cavalry Regiment, and the 25th Infantry

Division. We shared stories and spoke of home.

One of the guys from the 1st Cavalry had been wounded in the side of the head. One of his ears was partially missing. He told us about a firefight he was in at a firebase. The gooks had hit them very hard and had penetrated their perimeter. He had been shot by a gook with an AK-47 rifle. My goodness, he sure was lucky. He kept telling us how lucky he was to even be alive. He wanted to get back to his unit.

The food was very good. The doctors and male nurses took good care of me.

Note: no female nurses were there (darn).

Just lying there gave me time to think about home and recognizing how good I had it. I also thought about the guys still in the bush. I felt guilty sleeping on a cot, in a tent, out of the weather and out of harm's way. I wanted to get well quickly and rejoin the unit.

On May 11th, I was still in the hospital ward tent. I recall going to the "pisser" to take a leak. I looked to my left and there were several green body bags lying in a row. About five feet away was a body bag. It had a dead American soldier in it. The body bag was still open and I could see the soldier's arm sticking up and part of his face. He was fair skinned with red hair and freckles. It scared the hell out of me. I can still see him today, although the image in my mind is blurred. That was my first time seeing a dead American soldier and it made me realize this war was for real.

On May 12th, we experienced a heavy nighttime ground attack at Quan Loi. It must have been around 2200 hours (10 pm) when all hell broke loose on one side of the perimeter, which was about 300 meters from the hospital. That night, we in the hospital tent had to set up a perimeter around the area. There were about 15 of us. It was a terrible night with all the firing going on. Helicopters were in the air firing.

We could hear the sound of heavy machine gun and small arms fire from the perimeter. We could hear explosions throughout the base. We could see red tracer rounds going out and a few green tracer rounds coming in. We could hear in-coming rounds and lots of out-going rounds. Some aircraft sitting at the airfield were blown up. The Artillery was putting illumination rounds over the base camp. We could hear track vehicles moving to support the perimeter.

Though there were lots of shadows, we could see fairly well all around us as the illumination rounds were quite bright and there were a lot of them. We saw gooks running about 50 meters from our little perimeter and opened fire with our M16's. This was my first time seeing the enemy alive and moving. I fired as I saw them move. The Sergeant in charge kept telling us to be vigilant. We were being careful not to fire at our own guys. It was wild. We were geared up: eyes wide open. My heart was pounding.

We killed two gooks. They were "Sappers" (North Vietnamese Army or Vietcong Demolition Commandos) who had made it that far inside Quan Loi. The Sergeant instructed me and two other soldiers to go and check out one of the dead gooks. I followed orders, but I sure was scared. We slowly approached and found the gook was literally cut in half from being hit so many times by small arms fire. He had his satchel charge (explosives) still strapped to his upper body. That was my second time seeing a dead gook. Many soldiers were brought in that night. There were many dead and wounded. I knew Alpha Company was involved. The hospital sat close to the airstrip. We could see two aircraft smoldering where they had burned. We remained in our perimeter.

At daylight on May 13th, the firing had ceased. I was sent back to my unit. I walked back to our Company area. William Wright, Supply, instructed me to go with him. I rode with him in a deuce-and-a-half. We went to our Mortar Platoon's bunker. Bob Childers from Odessa, Texas, James (Butch) Marx of Sellersville, Pennsylvania, and Tom Drake, Ann Arbor, Michigan, were also there. We were part of a detail that dug three bodies out of a bunker the day after the ground attack. These soldiers were killed when a "Sapper," who had gotten through the wire, blew up their bunker. I wasn't very familiar with these guys, as I was new to the unit and they were in the Mortar Platoon.

It was still smoldering when we got there. We dug with our hands and carefully with entrenching tools to find the bodies. The Chaplain was with us and kept giving us encouragement to handle the situation and make sure we recovered these guys. One was burned beyond recognition. His entire body was burned except for the lower half of one leg. Part of his pant leg and his boot were still intact. It just didn't seem real. He didn't even appear to be human. I kept thinking that I didn't want to be burned to death like this poor guy. I convinced myself that he died instantly from the explosion and burned after he had died.

It was a terrible detail, but had to be done. The other two soldiers were found in the rubble. They were burned somewhat, but not like the first soldier. Digging these guys out of the dirt, wood and metal and handling their bodies was a real challenge for all. The Chaplain held prayer right then and there.

Today, I still carry a vivid picture in my mind of these three soldiers.

After this gruesome detail, Bob Childers and I reported back to the Company Area and found our Platoon. When I saw Sergeant Rilling, Lieutenant Zazarro and Vazanna they were relieved. Lieutenant Zazarro told me he didn't know if I was dead or alive, as we had suffered so many killed and wounded. He had heard the gooks had made it well inside the perimeter and that the hospital had been involved in the fight. Lieutenant Zazarro, Sergeant Rilling and Vazanna were very distraught. I just knew it was bad from the look on their faces. I couldn't believe it when they told me we had lost eleven. It was undetermined, at the time, the number of wounded. Included in the killed were Demings, Freeman and Gray. Fellow soldiers, who I knew, who had helped me, were killed. I was in shock. I was completely stunned. I just couldn't believe they were gone. They were gone forever. It just wouldn't register in my mind. I had never felt like this before. Demings was carrying my ammo cans. He had taken my place. This burden has weighed heavily on my mind and heart all these years.

That night, a couple of us guys were having a beer and I made a statement of how bad and rough the fighting had been. Another soldier—I can't remember his name — overheard our conversation and walked up and told me to shut the hell up as I wasn't even there with the Company and didn't know what I was talking about. I just let it go. There was no need for me to explain anything to anyone. Each of us had our own events that night and the next day and our own thoughts. I felt sorry for him, as I knew he was suffering from the losses.

Note: The night of May 12, 1969 we lost eleven soldiers who were killed and I never heard how many wounded, but there were several. That was the worst single event for A Company, 1st Battalion, 2nd Infantry Regiment in Vietnam. I just want to mention that I have been to the "Wall" in Washington, DC, visited the traveling "Wall" when it was in Nicholasville, KY and I visited the Vietnam Memorial in Morganton, NC. Each time, I thanked the guys and said a special prayer for them. I have also visited the on-line Virtual Wall. In May 2013, I had the honor of meeting Earnest Freeman's three sisters (Gladys Ross, Grace Robinson and Virginia Lefevers) and visiting his gravesite. It was very emotional, but most rewarding time for me.

On May 14th, we assembled the Company, the Chaplain held a prayer service, and we moved to the jungle. We were told it was better to get back to work and not dwell on our losses. I do recall how so few of us were going to the jungle. It's pure speculation on my part, but I think we must have had at least 30 in the Company wounded the night of May 12th. We were really short-handed. Many wounded never returned to our unit. I kept thinking how many we had lost and wondering about the wounded. I was hoping that we would get some much-needed replacements. Bob Faubert from California, who was wounded that night, rejoined the unit about three months later. He was a good guy, and I have had the honor of talking with Bob this past year.

We patrolled and set up ambushes every night. I was told the key was to keep the enemy moving and on its toes. We again made contact with the enemy outside of Quan Loi. Another soldier (I can't remember who it was, but he was a Private like me) and I were told to use C4 and detonation cord to blow trees out of the way to make an opening big enough to land a chopper for resupply and some wounded troops. The wounded were not critical, we were told. Remember, we had very little training using C4.

We knew to wrap the detonation cord around the tree where we wanted it to be cut off. How much, is what we didn't understand. Was it one wrap for every inch of tree diameter? Or was it two wraps? I think we went with three or four for good measure.

We had finished identifying the trees and wrapping the detonation cord. It was quite a large area. We hooked up the detonators, and yelled, "Fire in the hole!" three times, then set off the explosion.

And what an explosion it was!

We hit the ground and covered up. We were covered with leaves and debris. The Company was about 100 meters away and we blew large chunks of wood all over the place. Troops were hitting the ground and screaming out, "What the hell!" The trees didn't just fall, as we planned, but were blown up and away from their stubs. We really rattled the entire area and sent up a large bellowing cloud of dirt and debris. My first thought was, *OOOPS.* My second thought was, *I hope no one is hurt.* My third thought was, *our leaders are not going to be very happy.*

After everything settled down, I reported back to the Platoon CP. Lieutenant Zazarro asked, "Private Fair, do you think you used enough C4?"

I had nothing to say.

That was all that was said.

They will never ask me to do that detail again, I thought.

I watched Cartwright and learned how to use the heat tablets, provided to us to heat our rations, as a way to get the body warm and help dry out our clothes. We dug a small hole in the ground, placed the heat tablet in the hole and lit the tablet. We would sit on our "pots" (steel helmets) and cover our body and the hole with our poncho. The heat buildup inside would be great and warm the body right up and help dry our fatigues. You had to allow a vent opening at the back of your neck to allow the heat to escape. I was amazed how cold we got, especially at night, when it rained and we became completely soaked. The poncho and poncho liner were our saviors. The steel "pot" was also used as a washbasin. You removed the helmet liner, folded back the cover and poured in the water. It was great for washing and shaving.

One time we approached a large open area. It was too far to go around so Roger Johnson from Minnesota (I am sure it was Johnson) and I were sent across the open area to secure the other side. I handed my ammunition cans to another troop and Roger and I moved out.

I assumed it was our turn to face a high-risk situation. It was about 400—500 meters across the open area. When we got to the middle of the open area we came under fire from the far tree line. It was a machine gun that opened up on us. Luckily, when we hit the ground we were not hit. I remember seeing the green tracers from the machine gun go in between Roger and me. It was a terrifying moment. I think I may have wet my pants a little. Fortunately, we had crawled into a wet area. The front of my clothes was soaked so you couldn't tell.

We were able to crawl to an old bomb or artillery crater (defilade position), about two meters away, which allowed us to be lower than the machine gun rounds. Artillery was called in on the wood line and the gooks broke and ran. When we stood up, after the firing had ceased, I think some of our guys were surprised that we had not been hit. A lot of rounds had been fired at us.

The rest of the Platoon came out to us and we marched in line to the wood line. We got to where the gooks had set up, but they were gone. We found their fighting positions. There were empty bullet casings, some trash, and you could see where our artillery rounds had hit. I was still shaking.

Sometimes we would set up in a position and stay there for up to 24 hours. This provided some much needed additional rest. During this time troops occupied their time —when not on guard—with cleaning their weapons, personal hygiene, writing letters home, reading books and sleeping. It was also a time to reflect on life, family and friends. I would look at the sun or moon and think that my Mom, Dad, family and friends could see the same sun and moon that I was looking at. This allowed me to pause and consider that even though we were thousands of miles apart we were still close in one sense. It was a comforting thought. It was also an important time to take your boots off to allow your feet to air out. Foot powder, and using lots of it, was absolutely an essential in keeping your feet in good shape. We exercised extreme noise and light discipline to ensure we didn't give away our position.

That's about the time I learned what a F--K-you lizard was. It was a small lizard that made a sound very much like someone saying, "F--K-you." The small lizard would dig a small hole and use its head to pound the soil around the hole in place. It was neat to watch. Though, during the long nights the little lizard became an annoyance. Later on in years, I learned more about the lizard. The official name, I believe, is Tokay Gecko.

I also want to mention a plant in the bush that when touched, it would withdraw back. After a minute or so it would expand again. It was real strange to watch. I never knew what it was called.

Rain, rain, rain and more rain. The poncho would help at night, but during the day you just couldn't patrol with it on. When you are soaking wet for days and there's no let-up to the rain, you get cold, even in the jungle. Lying down at night in one to two inches of water didn't allow for much needed rest and sleep. We attempted to find an area with some incline to help keep the rain water flowing downhill and keep from forming puddles, but the rain was so heavy that many times the entire ground was just a huge puddle. Being wet all the time caused your hands, and especially your feet, to wrinkle and crack open. These were just more hardships we had to deal with. The rainy season in South Vietnam was May through September.

Let's not forget the mosquitos. Insect repellent (called bug juice by the troops) was another essential required to help ward off the mosquitos. During the day they were not as bad, but at night you had to fight them all night long. If you could avoid it, you never wanted to set up for the night near a stream or pond. There the mosquitos were at their worst. There were many sleepless nights. There were times, when we arose in the morning, that it was almost comical to see how swollen our faces and ears would be from all the mosquito bites. The "bug juice" just wasn't enough.

I started smoking, as the smoke helped to drive off the mosquitos. Cigarettes were included in the C-ration meals, so getting them was easy. I smoked unfiltered Lucky Strikes, Pall Mall and Camels, as these were the least favored by the troops; therefore they were abundant. I noted that many of our black soldiers preferred "Kools," which were a menthol cigarette. I didn't like the menthol. When I left Vietnam, I stopped smoking and haven't smoked since then.

And there were two other jungle monsters: leeches and red ants. If we crossed a stream we had to make sure we checked each other for leeches. There were small leaches (about the size of an ant) and some gigantic leaches (four to five inches long). Now there were many different ways to remove a leech. Just pulling it off was a no-no, as it left the head and that could cause an infection. Sticking the end of a burning cigarette to the leech caused the leech to let go, but when you are soaking wet with water dripping off you and your hands are wet it was difficult to hold or even light a cigarette. Then the last resort was to apply human urine. Evidently, the salt in the urine would cause the leech to let go. I can still recall peeing on my legs to get the leeches off, and if you were not watching closely other guys would slip up on you and pee on you also. We had a big laugh out of this. Can you imagine a guy holding his private parts and running over, trying to pee on another guy? Again, we got a good laugh out of all this.

Let's talk about those darn red ants. They would form a cocoon out of leaves that hung down from a tree or bush. There would be hundreds of these ants in these cocoons. As we walked through the jungle, we would bump into these cocoons and stir up the ants. There were many times the cocoon would fall down onto the rucksacks we carried. The ants would then attack the soldier and wow was it painful! The ants had large pincers and would deliver a painful bite. Now, think of hundreds of ants biting all at once. It was a sight to see how fast a soldier could strip and how his buddies would start slapping and picking ants off him. I believe I set the record time for going from fully clothed and with all my gear to completely naked in the jungle, jumping up and down and slapping at ants. I even got out of my boots and socks, as the ants were everywhere on me. After it was all over, we would have a good laugh. Even if you were the one under attack by the ants, you could still laugh about it especially after the guys told you what you looked like and how fast you were taking equipment and clothing off.

Mail call was a most important event for all soldiers. Receiving letters from home was a crucial part in helping all to make it through each day. Mail call, while we were in the bush, was with each resupply chopper that came every third day. I really felt for the married guys as you could tell it weighed heavily on them being away from their wives and, for some, children. Fortunately for me, I didn't have a girlfriend while I was in Vietnam. Not that I couldn't get a girl (some would argue this point) but I wanted it that way. Soldiers could send letters and post cards home for free. We just had to write "Free" in the upper right hand corner of the envelope or postcard. Our return address was our rank, name, unit and an APO address of San Francisco. It was a really nice benefit from the U.S. government.

My father was a man who showed very little emotions. He was not a hugging and kissing type person, and it was difficult for him to really get close to anyone. He was a good man, a good provider and a good father. I received a letter from my father (the one and only one I got from him) that really moved me emotionally. My father told me how much he loved me, how proud he was of me and how he longed for my safe return to the farm. I was in tears.

Cartwright asked, "Hey buddy, are you okay?"

I replied, "I'm fine."

This letter reminded me of the day I left home, heading to Vietnam. Wendell Rainwater, one of my best friends, came to pick me up to take me to the airport in Louisville. I said goodbye to Mom and little brother. Mom was in tears. I kept telling her over and over, that I would be fine and that I would see her in one year. Dad was outside in the barn lot working on some equipment. Mom had told me that he wouldn't come to the house when I was leaving.

As I got into the car, I shouted at Dad, "I'll see you in one year! You take care."

When dad looked up and just waved, I saw that he was in tears. This was the first time I ever saw my Dad cry. I was also in tears. When the car pulled away, I looked over my shoulder, through the rear window. And there was Dad, standing in the middle of the road watching as the car disappeared. I will never forget that mental picture burned in my mind. I just wanted to be half the man my Dad was.

Wendell asked, "Are you okay?"

I replied, "I'm okay. I hope Mom and Dad are okay. I'm sure going to miss them."

Wendell assured me, "They'll be just fine".

Mail kept us connected to our home and family, kept us going, but there were other necessary items that kept us going too. Iodine tablets were essential and had to be carried. The canteen cover had a small side pocket designed just for the small iodine tablet bottle. We used a lot of water while in the hot jungle. We carried a lot of water, but never enough. So when we obtained water from a stream, bomb crater or even from a puddle, we would put iodine tablets into the water to make it safe to drink. One tablet was used for clear water. Two tablets were used for slightly dingy water, three to four tablets for muddy water. You just waited about 15 minutes and the water was safe to drink. It didn't taste good, but it was wet and a thirst quencher. Iodine tablets were a lifesaver.

I was assigned the M60 machine gun. At first, I was overcome by being selected to handle the heavy firepower for the Platoon. I knew how to disassemble and reassemble the M60 and do it in a hurry (great training at Ft. Polk, LA). I was also trained to shoot in six to nine round bursts and how to watch for overheating of the barrel. I soon learned how it kicked my butt in the boonies. I recall Sergeant Fuqua, black handle bar mustache, talking with me while we were in the bush. He made a comment about how I was carrying my M60 and suggested folding out one leg of the bi-pod as a handle. It worked as it helped me to balance the M60 on my shoulder as we marched through the bush. The M60 weighed about 23 pounds, and with a 100 round belt fed into the cover it weighed about 30 pounds. It fired 600 rounds per minute with every fifth round a red tracer. It was the firepower of the Platoon. Two men were assigned to each M60 Gunner: an Assistant Gunner and an Ammo Bearer. Both carried two cans of 7.62 MM ammo for the M60 and one carried a spare barrel. At the time, Edward Lewis, a black guy from Mississippi and John Sutton from West Virginia were with me. Believe me, that darn M60 managed to snag on every limb and vine in the jungle, and there were plenty of them.

I was also issued a Colt .45 pistol. Machine Gunners carried the Colt .45 for close protection in case the M60 jammed or your position was being overrun. More weight to be carried. I thought if I have to use the pistol I was in a world of sh-t. I hate to admit it, but I did fire the pistol a few times when we were in contact with the enemy and everyone was firing. I pointed in the direction of the enemy and fired. I wasted ammunition. I just wanted to make sure it would fire okay. Of course, I had to clean it after the firing ceased.

Another day we were in heavy contact with the enemy. We were working with a Mechanized Infantry Company of the 2nd Battalion, 2nd Infantry Regiment, known as our sister battalion. I believe their nickname was the "Iron Fist." They were a great unit! We had formed a company size skirmish line across a large grassy open area with the Mechanized unit to our left. We were well spread out. The grass was about waist high. There was heavy firing from all around us. I was firing my M60 heavily and staying in line with the troops. My M60 jammed. Sergeant Rilling, Sutton, Lewis and another troop and I stopped and I had to remove the butt plate and the bolt assembly. Evidently, when I opened the cover to place another belt of ammo in the tray, a link fell down into the receiver. I got the machine gun operational again, but just in the few minutes we stopped, the line of troops had moved well away from us.

In the tall grass, we couldn't see that far to our front unless we stood up. We crouched and moved forward and found the unit had been split by all the enemy fire and confusion. There was no longer a line of troops in our direct front. Some troops were confused and moving back toward us. Some were down and crawling. Sergeant Rilling ordered all that we saw to form a new line toward the enemy. He told everyone to hold their ground and be extra cautious as our own troops could be moving back to us. Sergeant Rilling took charge and was an excellent leader.

A guy had settled in next to us. He had been firing his M16 and it was hot. He had it pointed outward. Another troop came crawling up to his position in the tall grass and just as he came up a round was "cooked off" in the M16. It just missed this guy's head. He received powder burns on the side of his face, his ear was ringing and he was scared out of his mind. Sergeant Rilling had everyone point their weapons up just in case there were more troops crawling toward our positions.

Finally, contact with the gooks was broken and the firing ceased. The Company started re-grouping. We rejoined our Squad and Platoon. That was one lucky troop.

Note: the M60 never has a cook-off, as a round is not chambered when not firing. Once chambered, the round fires and the bolt comes back to the open position. I don't know what became of the soldier. We did have some wounded who were taken out by MEDEVAC. He may have been one of them.

There were terrifying moments that made your heart pound exceptionally hard in your chest and your body to shake all over. I felt my heart would explode and I couldn't control the shaking. It is hard for me to express how it felt to be so afraid. The fear of death so close at hand just can't be easily described.

It is strange what can run through one's mind during all the heavy fighting we were involved in during the last few weeks. I thought perhaps getting wounded would be a blessing, if the wound was not so severe as to cause a permanent disability. I didn't want to lose a limb or my eyesight. I guess I was looking for a million dollar wound. That's what they called it when you got wounded and they sent you back to the United States. I soon overcame those thoughts. I convinced myself that was a cowardly way to think. I was ashamed that I had even thought of such things.

I kept thinking about how easy it was to become close with my fellow soldiers, but how difficult it was to see them wounded or die. I had heard stories of soldiers not wanting to make friends with anyone and I could easily understand why, but my human nature wouldn't allow me not to become friends.

When the resupply choppers came out they would bring us soft drinks and blocks of ice along with clothing, water, rations, and ammunition. We would strip off our dirty fatigues and grab clean ones brought to us. The key was finding your size. The uniforms were all in two or three big piles. I recall wearing my pants far too large and having to bundle them up around my belt just to keep them from falling down. Usually, the shirts were not a problem unless they were far too small. This was called DX, or direct exchange of the uniform.

The soft drinks were hot and the guys showed me how to roll a can of soft drink on a block of ice to cool it real quick. It worked, and you could see a lot of guys doing the "roll."

If we needed something we just wrote it down and gave it to the supply guy who came out with the supply chopper: boots, belts, bug repellent, foot powder, writing paper, ink pens, equipment, etc. Our supply guys did their best to make sure our needs were met. Many thanks to our RTO's (Radio/Telephone Operators) for they kept lists of what the troops needed and called the items in via the radio so the supply guys could get them on the supply chopper.

Outside of Lai Khe we were working with the 11th ACR and the 1st Squadron, 1st Battalion 4th Cavalry Regiment (Quarter Horse). There was sporadic fire all day long. Here the rubber plantation was quite young with small trees. We had an M113 get hit by an RPG (rocket propelled grenade). Fortunately, it was hit in such a way that there were no casualties. It was not on a road, but deep in the rubber trees. All the equipment was removed from the APC. It was left and blown in place. When the C4 went off, it was quite the explosion. That APC was blown apart like it was paper.

The next day, I was riding with my entire Squad on an M48 tank on a road leading to Lai Khe. The tank just in front of us hit a land mine. I was amazed at how large the crater was that had been blown beneath the tank. The driver received an ear injury from the noise. The track and some road wheels were blown off. Luckily no one else was injured, just shaken up real bad. Engineers were called in and swept the road for mines. An M88 recovery vehicle was hooked up to the M48 tank and it literally dragged the M48 tank with one side of the track off all the way back to Lai Khe, which must have been 3-4 miles.

There was a guy I had met at the Communications Center in Lai Khe. I can't recall his name. From there, he gave me the chance to call home using the FM radios. I was told the radio "skip" was running well and that FM radio calls could be made. Vietnam was 13 hours ahead of Eastern Standard Time in the US. I was able to contact a Ham Radio Operator in Louisiana. I asked him to use the telephone and call my home phone in Campbellsville, Kentucky. He would hold the FM mike to the telephone receiver and I could talk to my parents.

I told him to call collect, and my parents would accept the charges. He told me that the least he could do was to pay for the charges.

My Mom and Dad were not home, but my younger brother, Terry, who was 11 years old at the time, was there. I got to talk to him briefly and I told him I was doing fine. He told me all was well at home. Then we lost the "skip" and the call ended. I never knew who the Ham Operator was, but I still thank him today. Later on, I found out that my parents didn't believe my brother when he told them I had called. They thought he was only trying to make them feel better. When I came home from Vietnam, I mentioned the call to Mom and Dad. They were astounded, and thought my brother had made it up all this time.

In the bush, when "mother nature" called and you had to urinate or have a bowel movement, it was quite easy. When we had to urinate, we just walked off from the others a short distance and found a tree or bush and let it go. If you had to have a bowel movement, you walked off a short distance, found a tree or bush, dug a small hole using the entrenching tool, and squatted down and took a dump. Then you covered it up. The key was letting the other guys know you were taking care of business and making sure you took your weapon with you. Getting caught with your pants down would not be very good. If you didn't have a weapon, it was even worse. Toilet paper came in each meal of C-rations. You always saved the toilet paper.

We were in a Company defensive position in the middle of the day when two gooks walked into our perimeter. Our Squad didn't see them, but all of a sudden firing broke out. We hit the ground, but we didn't fire, as we didn't know where to fire and what we were firing at. It was most intense for less than a minute. When it settled down, Davis noted that a round had hit the magazine in his M16. Now that was close. It must have gotten hit while it was stacked on top of his rucksack, which was on the ground. Later, we were told about the two gooks, in full NVA uniform and gear, walking inside our perimeter. One was thought for sure to be an officer. They fired off some rounds and ran like hell. They escaped.

One of the guys leaving Vietnam gave me a camera and some film. It was a 104 Instamatic. I can't recall his name, but I sure thank him. The camera was small, lightweight and easy to use. It fit perfectly into an ammo pouch. I kept it wrapped in plastic. Later on, my mom sent me lots of film for it. I decided I needed to take photos of all the guys I was serving with. I wanted the photos to remember them by. I am so glad I did. Other troops also took lots of photos and I had them provide me copies. Today, I have several hundred photos. They are priceless.

We moved into FSB Pine Ridge that had been abandoned for several months by the 1st Cavalry Division or 25th Infantry Division. As Alpha Company moved up to the perimeter, we were lined up and told to lay down fire into the abandoned base just in case there were any dinks inside. I fired my M60 and spent over 300 rounds into the base. Hell, I shot up the latrine, shower and bunkers. When we moved in all the soldiers were complaining about how much damage we had done firing up the place, especially the showers. The large drums that held the shower water were shot full of holes. SP4 Chiser, a black guy from Chicago, was laughing at me and kept saying how great a job I had done shooting up all the good stuff. He was a real great guy with a great sense of humor and my friend.

As we continued to occupy the firebase and clean things up, Jim Click found a small snake and placed it in a sandbag. He wanted to show everyone what he had caught, thinking it was pretty cool. He took the snake to the Company CP (Command Post). Ron Hume from Texas and Doc Taylor from Utah were there. Doc Taylor opened the sandbag, quickly dropped it on the ground and stomped it several times, killing the snake. Doc Taylor calmly explained to Click that he was certain that he had caught a bamboo viper. It's a highly venomous snake and not one to play around with. The word got out and the rest of the troops were extremely careful in cleaning up the area. We were all reluctant to get inside the bunkers.

FSB Pine Ridge was situated on top of a mountain range we called the "Razor Backs." From there, you could see Tay Ninh City in the far distance. We could also see Nui Ba Den (the Black Virgin Mountain) in the far distance. It was a neat firebase and was easy to defend, as all around the perimeter was a fairly sharp drop off.

We witnessed a B52 bomb run from FSB Pine Ridge. It was amazing to watch and hard to believe how much ordnance fell from the air into a large strip of jungle. The next day we got to see the damage first hand as we were directed to patrol the area that had been bombed. What a mess it was. No person could have survived being in the bombed area. It was difficult to walk through the muck and downfall. We patrolled areas that had been sprayed with Agent Orange. It was amazing to see all the dead vegetation. It was really strange.

When we would fly over areas that had been bombed by B52's, it looked like potholes all over the landscape. Thousands and thousands of bombs had been dropped. The areas were really devastated.

I recall when Staff Sergeant Michael Schellenberger joined our unit. I believe it was the last part of May, and at FSB Song Be. His nickname was Shelly. He was from Jeffersonville, Indiana, which is about 90 miles from my hometown of Campbellsville, KY. He was what the soldiers called a "Shake and Bake" NCO. He had gone through the Non-Commissioned Officer Academy right after AIT and made NCO. He didn't make it through the normal method; he bypassed E-4 and E-5. Some troops didn't have much respect for these type NCO's, but Shelly proved he was a very qualified and capable leader, very rapidly. He was a darn good Platoon Sergeant (PSG) and was well respected by all. We became very good friends. I met Shelly and Jeff Mill in Louisville in 1972. Shelly and I have met since then a couple of times. It is an honor to meet with him.

On May 27th, November Platoon landed in a hot LZ (Landing Zone). Lieutenant Alphonzo Chavis from North Carolina, and SP4 Kenneth Smith from Michigan, along with a Vietnamese Scout, were killed. We were, I believe, at FSB Song Be—this is not clear. Lima and Mike Platoons were called out to go in and retake the LZ. There were troops pinned down. Everyone was anxious to get moving to help our brothers. We were afraid, but there was no way any of us were not going. We were loaded up on M113 APC's (armored personnel carriers) with the Headquarters Company of 2nd Battalion and moved to the hot LZ. Contact had mainly been broken with only sporadic fire. We formed a skirmish line and moved across the open field. We were moving with extreme caution just waiting to be fired on from the wood line. Vazanna, Sutton, and another soldier and I found Lieutenant Chavis, Smith and the Scout. They were lying together in the tall grass. I recall seeing a bandage applied to the backside of Lieutenant Chavis' neck. He was lying on his side. I couldn't see any wounds on Smith or the Scout. Smith was lying face down. The Scout was lying face up and his eyes were frozen open.

We knew they were dead.

All of a sudden, a gook fired an RPG from the wood line and we all hit the ground and commenced firing on the wood line. The round went over our heads and hit in the wood line behind us. No one was injured. There was heavy firing from our left, and we could hear the M113's laying down a wall of fire into the wood line. Firing ceased and contact was broken. We scurried to the wood line and formed a defensive perimeter just inside the wood line. We were told to rest. I fell asleep, and when Vazanna woke me up, I couldn't believe I had slept two solid hours. It was like I had been drugged. It seemed just like a few minutes. I guess my adrenaline had flowed so hard and fast that my body was in a pure exhaustive state.

I didn't know at the time that two soldiers from Headquarters Company, 2nd Battalion, 1LT James Clark,

Nevada and PFC Henry Hausman, Ohio had been killed during the firefight. Their APC was hit heavily with small arms fire. I remember helping to load the five bodies in the M113's and riding on top as we moved back to the firebase. I was riding on the M113 that held SP4 Smith's body. I remember looking down at SP4 Smith, who was wrapped in a poncho, and wondering about his family. I didn't know him that well, me being fairly new to the unit, and he was in another platoon. I said a prayer for him. At a time like this, the question that comes to one's mind is, "Am I next?"

I can still see him clearly in my mind today.

If we were at a firebase, there were many nights that a platoon or sometimes a squad was sent out to set up an ambush. The Company leaders attempted to make sure this detail was divided up equally and no one Platoon or Squad did more than the others. Troops fairly knew whose turn it was, and for sure if it was or wasn't their turn. It could be terrifying, and was a very high-risk detail.

Sergeant Nugent, a Squad Leader in our Platoon, got in a heap of trouble at FSB Song Be. His Squad was ordered to set up an ambush outside of Song Be. The Squad was ordered to leave just before dark and get the ambush set up by dark. There had been reports of a lot of enemy movement in our area. All was well until Captain Scully was walking the perimeter that night, heard a radio break squelch and found that the Squad had set up in a bunker at the gate. They were using the radio and calling back Sit-Reps (situation reports) just as if they were at the ambush site. Sergeant Nugent had disobeyed a direct order. Captain Scully went off and from what I overheard there was going to be hell to pay.

The story made its way around the entire Company. I really felt sorry for Sergeant Nugent, as I could reasonably understand why they had not gone out and set up the ambush. The last month had been hell on everyone in our Company. We had lost a lot of good men, the area was saturated with NVA and Viet Cong, everyone was worn out and depressed and, let's face it, they were afraid. I would be too.

Captain Scully pursued the maximum punishment. Later, after the investigation and court martial, Sergeant

JOE FAIR

Nugent was reduced in rank and moved to Mike Platoon. He remained with Mike Platoon until he was severely wounded in the thigh in August and sent back stateside. He was a good man.

Chapter Three

June 1969

I was cleaning my Colt .45 pistol at Song Be. When I had finished cleaning the pistol, I was checking to make sure it worked well and inserted a magazine. I pulled the receiver to the rear, released it, pointed the pistol out the bunker firing port toward the perimeter and pulled the trigger. I forgot I had a round chambered. Of course, the pistol fired, and it scared the hell out of me. I quickly unloaded and cleared my pistol. I just sat there. All in the Platoon had hit the ground and were looking to see what the firing was all about. I thought, *oh no.* It may have been Staff Sergeant Schellenberger, though I am not sure which leader, who came to the bunker and asked what happened. I, with egg on my face and blood red with embarrassment, had to explain I had accidentally fired the pistol. I believe I was called "Barney Fife" for the next few days. I took it with good stride and moved on.

Another unusual event took place while I was cleaning my M60 machine gun at Song Be. I was sitting on my poncho and had all the parts spread out. I had the receiver group across my lap. A helicopter had just landed. I kept on cleaning. I didn't pay any attention to the helicopter landing, which occurred almost hourly. Then, I noticed a very highly polished set of boots right next to my poncho. When I looked up, I could see it was an important, high-ranking individual. I was attempting to jump up, but the man told me to stay seated. I stared and in disbelief, recognized the 4 stars of a General. I was stunned. I read the nametag and it said, "Abrams."

It was General Creighton Abrams!

He was the overall leader of all Armed Forces in Vietnam. At the time, I didn't know who he was. All I knew was he was a General. He asked where I was from and I told him Kentucky. He said that's the home of Armor at Ft.

Knox, Kentucky. I can't recall my reply. He then said, "Take care, young man."

I said, "Yes, sir."

He had a large entourage of high-ranking soldiers with him. That was the highlight of my day. The guys were again giving me a hard time and said I was really kissing some "big time" ass. I just laughed it off.

Unexploded ordinance was dangerous and not to be messed with. Lima Platoon was patrolling the bush outside of Dau Tieng and had stopped for a rest period. A new guy, walking close to the point man, picked up two shiny objects he found lying on the ground and brought them back to the Platoon CP (Command Post) to show Lieutenant Zazarro and Bob Childers, who was the lieutenant's RTO. Not knowing what they were, Lieutenant Zazarro pitched them aside into the bush. All of a sudden, one exploded!

Bob Childers was close enough that the explosion threw him backwards and onto the ground. Bob received shrapnel to the upper chest and a neck injury from the fall. The new guy (I can't recall his name) had an ear injury. Luckily, we were very close to an open area. MEDEVAC was called in and Bob and the new guy were flown to the hospital in Dau Tieng. A few days later, they returned to the unit. Their injuries were not severe.

The two objects were unexploded bomb-lets from a cluster bomb dropped by the US Air Force. A cluster bomb is a bomb containing multiple explosive sub-munitions (bomb-lets). These bombs are dropped from aircraft or fired from the ground and designed to break open in mid-air, releasing the sub-munitions and saturating an area that can be the size of several football fields. Anybody within that area is very likely to be killed or seriously injured. We all learned a valuable lesson that day; leave the unknown alone.

Roger Johnson had so much bamboo poisoning on his arms that both arms were wrapped at the Battalion Aid Station from elbow to hand with white bandages. Now that went over well, as he had to move out again to the jungle. White bandages were not very good camouflage. He had to remove the white bandages, which was, oh, so good for the healing process. The Company Commander was not going to give him an excuse to remain at the firebase. Roger didn't want it anyway. He was a tough soldier.

Sometime in early June, perhaps late May, Captain Coker, our new Company Commander, Lieutenant Holtz, our new Platoon Leader, and First Sergeant Cabrera joined our Company. Captain Thomas Coker was from Colorado and Lieutenant Jay Holtz was from Oregon. I didn't know where "Top" was from. I am guessing he was from Puerto Rico. They turned out to be great leaders and earned our respect very quickly. I never knew what happened with Captain Scully.

Lieutenant Zazarro became the Company Executive Officer (XO) for a period of time and later went to our Battalion or Brigade Headquarters and was assigned to the PX. Lieutenant Zazarro was a superb Platoon Leader. He had seen a lot of action and witnessed the death of several Lima Platoon soldiers. Sergeant Rilling had done his year tour and returned home to the states. He was a good man and a darn good NCO. I hated to see him leave, but I was also happy for him.

Lieutenant Colonel Winfield Holt was the new Battalion Commander. I remember later on that he came to the bush and patrolled with our unit and spent the night with us in a company size NDP. He was a rather tall and slender man. He was armed with a Colt .45 and he seemed to me a very serious, genuine person just from the way he carried himself. I felt he was a very good Commander, from what little I knew and had seen of him. From what I heard, he had seen action in Korea.

It was anxious times when lying in the bush at night and hearing the B52 Bombers dropping their bombs quite close by and praying they knew where we were and where they were. You could hear the distant roar of the B52 engines and then the high pitch squeal of the bombs as they were released and fell to earth. The rumble from all the bombs going off was astounding. I would sometimes attempt to imagine what it would be like to be on the receiving end of a B52 bomb run. I knew our enemy had gone through this.

It was interesting seeing the Cobra gunships using their mini-guns at night and the solid red tracer lines and the buzz sound from the rapid firing. Every night in the bush there was also artillery-firing going on. The big 175mm cannon, the big 8-inch gun, 105 howitzers and mortars would virtually fire all night. Illumination rounds were fired and when they burst in the air overhead you could hear the sound of the canister as it passed through the air and fell to the ground. When artillery rounds were fired close to our positions you could actually hear the buzz from the shrapnel as it went through the air. That was frightening. Again, when it was being fired fairly close to your position you would lie there and hope the rounds didn't land on top of you.

One of the guys in my Squad had torn part of a small photo out of a Playboy magazine. It was a photo of a rather large set of female breasts. He had stuck that in the back of my steel pot under the camouflage band. I didn't know it was there. First Sergeant Cabrera was patrolling with us. As I walked by him he asked, "Fair, what the hell have you got stuck in your helmet band?"

I replied, "My P38 can opener Top."

He said, "You ain't going to open many cans with that. Take it out now!"

I removed my helmet and saw the photo. I looked at Top, shook my head and just laughed.

He didn't smile or say anything else, but I was for certain he knew that I had been had by one of the guys. I think I saw him smile as he turned away from me. I looked back at Sutton and Strickland, with a frown on my face, but they just smiled real big. I asked myself were they really my good buddies? Then, I had to laugh.

It was comical when an officer approached the Squad that some of the guys would whisper "BOHICA." That translated to, "bend over, here it comes again." Usually, the officer was there to tell us about our next mission.

I remember Lewis, who was my Ammo Bearer, never would lie down in the bush. He always just sat on an ammo can and placed his head on his knees and slept that way. He refused to lay down where there were bugs. He was quiet but a great guy. He was very strong, well built and could hump ammo easily. He never complained about anything. He was my friend. I'd rib Lewis about being so quiet. I asked him, "Lewis why are you so quiet?"

He told me I did enough talking for the two of us. I am sure he was right.

During June, the Battalion moved its headquarters to Dau Tieng. From here we worked out of FSB Mahone and FSB Pine Ridge. We worked in the Michelin Rubber Plantation, the Iron Triangle and the surrounding jungle. If my memory serves me correctly, this was the first time the Company was loaded on a C130 airplane. The C130 was a turbo-prop plane that could take-off and land on short runways. I believe we flew from Song Be to Dau Tieng.

The Company, of about 100 men, was loaded onto one or two C130's. We sat on the floor of the plane and had straps every five to six feet strung between us. The pilot gave it full power with the brakes on then released the brakes. The plane lunged forward—we all slid to the rear—shot down the runway and then took off. Then we knew what the straps were for. When we landed, the pilot hit the runway and slammed on the brakes. We all slid forward. If it weren't for the straps, we would have been piled up at one end of the plane.

In June (as best I can remember) we started getting replacements. I recall Roy Bohn from Texas who came to us from the Engineers. I became a close friend with Bohn. In 1974, I met Roy in Houston. I was there on a business trip while working for Ingersoll Rand. Boy, it was sure good to see him. We had dinner and a few drinks together. I haven't seen Roy since then, but have talked to him on the phone. It is so comforting talking to these guys after all these years.

Other soldiers who joined our unit around this time were Jim Ward of Ohio, Jeff Mill from Connecticut, and Berl Martin from Iowa. These guys were excellent soldiers, tough as nails and became my friends.

The Battalion held a ceremony for all the soldiers who had been killed within the past few months. For each soldier who was killed, there was an M16 rifle with a bayonet stuck in the ground with a helmet placed on top of it. Also, a highly shined pair of boots was placed at the base of each rifle. There were 18 being honored.

Vazanna and a few others worked rigorously to get the boots spit shined. I helped with the cleaning of the rifles. We worked hard to make sure the rifles were spotless. A highly starched and pressed Black Scarf was placed on the M-16 rifle. We all stood at attention and saluted the memory of these fine men. Each man's name was announced with a moment of silence between each name. The Chaplain had prayer with us. It was a very moving ceremony and there were a lot of tears, yes even from grown, hard-ass men, like we portrayed ourselves to be.

When the names David Demings, Ronald Gray and Earnest Freeman were called, a picture of their faces went through my mind. I was moved and there was a hurting deep within my heart. I was choked up. I still just couldn't believe they had been killed. It was hard to believe we had lost eighteen men. Good, young men who had so much of their future still yet to live. Now, they were gone forever. I will never ever forget.

Many thanks to our Medics: Taylor, Fisk, Gayton and all the others I have, over time, forgotten. They helped to keep all of us healthy. They ensured we took our small white Malaria pill every day and the big orange pill once per week. They looked after our aches and pains, cuts and bruises, and our overall wellbeing. They would tell us to check our urine. If we were urinating and it was real yellow, we were not drinking enough water. Our urine needed to be clear. Our most common aliments were cuts, bruises, bacterial and fungal skin rashes, skin sores (the troops called bamboo poisoning), diarrhea, colds, headaches, ear infections, sprains and strains. Every now and then someone would get a case of the worms. Our medics didn't hesitate, even under heavy fire, to come to the aid of a wounded soldier. They were truly unsung heroes.

I received a rather bad chemical burn on my left hip from the insect repellent (bug juice) we carried. I had a bottle in my lower left shirt pocket and I didn't notice the top had cracked. The bug juice ran out and soaked my pants at my left hip. This created a chemical burn to my skin. I thank Doc Taylor for providing me some cream, applying bandages and checking on me each day. The burn soon healed after four or five days, but it was a real aggravation at the time. I still carry a scar from the burn. I have been in contact with Doc Taylor over the past year and it has been great.

I had a real good time watching a band from the Philippines playing country music at Dau Tieng. I was amazed when the lead singer started singing "Swinging Doors" by Merle Haggard and he sounded just like Merle. The band was really good. Then they performed "Silver Wings" and it was awesome. I recall that, "I Can't Get No Satisfaction," by the Rolling Stones was one of the number one hits in Vietnam.

Like I had previously noted, every soldier had a problem with ringworm and other skin rashes. We used bottle after bottle of Tinactin to help with the rash and the constant itching. When we stripped down, many of us were covered almost head to toe with some type of rash or skin problem. Under our uniforms many of the white guys were very fair skinned. All our faces, hands and arms were deeply tanned. I had a much darker complexion since my grandmother was one-half Cherokee Indian and I had some of her features. Of course, our Black and Hispanic comrades didn't have this tan problem. They would rib us about being so white. Chiser called me "chicken legs." I reminded him that I wasn't as white as some of the others.

When we were at Dau Tieng we had to, of course, pull guard duty at our assigned bunker along the base perimeter. Typically, it was Berl Martin, Edward Lewis, John Sutton, Joe Spruill, Charles Strickland and I. In front of our bunker, about 150 meters out, a Vietnamese Policeman (we called them "White Mice") had a small guard shack built on a major road to keep him out of the hot sun and the rain. His duty was checking traffic in and out of the city of Dau Tieng during the day. Two nights in a row we destroyed his little shack with M79 grenade rounds. Each morning when he came out to pull his duty, he would see the shack destroyed and give our bunker a Vietnamese cussing. It would take him a while to build the shack back. We would just laugh and enjoy the moment (GI's being GI's). Then a "Butter Bar" (2nd Lieutenant) came to our bunker and promised us that if the little guard shack was damaged the next morning there would be hell to pay. We didn't destroy the little shack after that.

We didn't need any more hell.

Bob Childers was an excellent RTO (Radio Telephone Operator) and a darn good soldier. I've had the honor to meet Bob in the past year. We stay in touch. He still had his note pad from June 1969 when we were patrolling in the Michelin Rubber Plantation. His note pad showed where he had written down the grid coordinates for our many positions and the supply list he was transmitting to the rear. What a piece of our history!

The entire Company traveled to Di An for a much needed three day stand-down. A stand down was a rest and relaxation period. No duty assignments. We had basketball courts and a swimming pool. There was also a modern mess hall and club. The mess hall was super nice. It was air conditioned, had curtains on the windows, and there were nice tables and chairs. We ate from trays and drank from glasses. The food was outstanding. It was almost like being stateside. We were reluctant to leave the cool air-conditioned room, so the Mess Sergeant had to run us out.

There were movies and a stage that had a rock band playing. I have some great photos of the band and the girls. I remember Rock Davis playing a piano they had at the club. He was talented. There was a guy in one of the other platoons, I can't recall his name, but was dynamite on the guitar and a great singer. We spent just about all night drinking beer and listening to him sing and play.

At the movies that night, a fight broke out between two rear echelon troops: a huge Spanish guy and the bouncer. The bouncer kicked the Spanish guy's butt real bad. The bouncer was about 6 feet tall and weighed about 180 pounds. But he was tough, fast and knew how to fight. I thought I didn't need to see GI's fighting GI's with all that we were going through. We were all on the same side. I felt that the guys in the rear needed to be assigned to an infantry line company to get all the aggression out of them.

The second day at Di An, the Brigade Sergeant Major (the Sergeant Major was the top ranking NCO in the

Brigade) had the metal box (we called a connex) opened where we had stored our weapons. Our weapons were dirty, rusty and piled haphazardly. The Sergeant Major had a "sh-t fit." We all had to retrieve our weapons and thoroughly clean, oil, and store them properly. The Sergeant Major was right, but at the time all we had on our minds was sleeping, beer and partying.

John Sutton and I went to the local steam bath and massage parlor, located at Di An, as we were told it was wonderful experience and very inexpensive. Two young country boys, one from Kentucky and one from West Virginia, going to such a place was something to really think about. We were told to completely undress and wrap a towel around our midsection by two Vietnamese ladies who worked at the parlor. They didn't leave the room. At that time, for me to undress in front of a female was almost too much for me to even think about doing but the ladies kept saying, "Me no look. You take clothes off. Wrap towel around you. You enjoy steam bath and massage."

John and I reluctantly did as we were instructed and sure enough the two ladies didn't look.

They put us in a steam box through a front door. The box also had a hole in the top of it that allowed our head to protrude out. Then they turned on the steam. Wow, at first I thought I was going to smother, but soon the steam felt good and my body was relaxing. After about ten minutes, they had us get out of the steam box and lay face down on a table. (We still had the towels around our midsections). Then the massage started, and boy was I relaxed. After the ten minutes in the hot steam bath, and now the fifteen-minute massage, I was calm and well relaxed.

After the massage, John and I were laughing as the two ladies (not very attractive and quite older than us) offered more than what we came for. They said, "Me make you really, really happy for ten dollar more. Me know how to make you feel oh so good."

Perhaps had they been young and attractive, I may have taken them up on their offer. John was married and didn't even consider it, as he was a faithful husband. We declined. We were laughing all the way back to the unit.

The guys asked us if we enjoyed the steam bath, massage and the little extra.

John and I just said, "Oh yeah."

The next day we moved back to Dau Tieng and then back to the bush. I can't recall how we got to Di An and back to Dau Tieng. It may have been by C130 fixed wing aircraft.

The 1st Engineering Battalion was scattered throughout the Division's area of operation and provided support for the units. They dug bunkers, erected towers, erected bridges across rivers and streams, built buildings and cleared areas for the artillery positions. Around the base camps and firebases the vegetation was cleared away from the perimeter by bulldozers that the Army called Rome Plows. These guys drove the plows right up to the edge of the jungle and were sitting ducks for the enemy. Several times our Company provided security detail while these guys worked the Rome Plows.

The Engineering unit also provided minesweeping and removal, which was dangerous work. These units were also home to the famous "Tunnel Rats." Armed with only a Colt .45, the "Tunnel Rats" went down into the tunnel systems looking for the enemy. Now that took courage. I think I was too tall to become a tunnel rat. I knew there was an advantage to being tall. I sure didn't want to crawl into one of those tunnels.

Chapter Four

July 1969

On July 7th, Staff Sergeant Thomas Sizemore was wounded by an incoming mortar or rocket round. He eventually died from his wounds. He had been assigned to Alpha Company from Battalion Headquarters for just a short time; therefore most of us didn't know him that well. I believe we were at FSB Thunder IV. I'm just not sure which firebase we were at.

I recall this quite well, as I was feeling really bad due to a head cold. One of the Medics gave me some Darvon and told me to get some much-needed rest. That evening, before dark, I took the Darvon and went inside the perimeter bunker my Squad was assigned to and went to sleep. The guys let me sleep all night and boy did I. The medicine must have been super strong, as we incurred incoming rounds at the firebase and I slept through it all. Sutton and Strickland kept jabbing me about sleeping through one hell of a ground attack and that they fought off wave after wave of gooks attacking our bunker. They told me they were put in for the Medal of Honor. Of course this wasn't true, as it was just a mortar and rocket attack. The troops had a saying: "Fairy tales start with 'Once upon a time' and war stories with 'This is no sh-t'." We were all concerned about Staff Sergeant Sizemore getting wounded. We had heard he was critical.

Here's the best list I could come up with of the men in 1st (Lima) Platoon at Dau Tieng during Mid-1969:

Lieutenant Holtz—Platoon Leader
Taylor —Medic
Schellenberger—Platoon Sergeant
Martin—4th Squad
Vazanna—3rd Squad
Strickland—4th Squad

Ward—2nd Squad
Sutton—4th Squad
Spruill—4th Squad
Sperry (Pappy)—2nd Squad
White—2nd Squad
Mill—1st Squad
Elsos—2nd Squad
Neumer—1st Squad
Montemayor—3rd Squad
Houston—1st Squad
McAdams—3rd Squad
Fair—4th Squad
Lewis—4th Squad
Bohn—2nd Squad
Chiser—3rd Squad
Koeppen—1st Squad
Johnson—4th Squad

There were three other guys, but I cannot remember their names. I hope I have the Squad assignments correct and that I have not missed anyone. I believe Bob Childers was the RTO for Captain Coker at this time. He was in the Company Command post and was not in our Platoon. I felt close to all these guys.

Berl Martin was another guy I remember quite well. He was from Iowa. He was short, stocky, and wore glasses. He was not married. He wore a peace sign emblem around his neck, and when he waved at you it was always with the two finger peace sign. It seemed to me that he was always happy. He carried ammo then moved to the radio. He was a good man, a good friend and a tough soldier. I've had the pleasure of talking with Berl by phone.

While flying in a chopper going out to the bush, I had my legs and my M60 machine gun hanging out the door (John Wayne style). All of a sudden, I felt my M60 get a lot lighter and when I looked down the barrel had come off and was falling back to the ground. I could see the barrel spiraling as it rapidly dropped to the ground. The vibration from the chopper caused the barrel to come loose. We were probably at 2,000 feet. I looked up and Lieutenant Holtz was looking at me and shaking his head. Boy, I sure felt like an idiot. Luckily, the Door Gunner saw what happened and handed me a spare barrel. Later, I found the barrel locking mechanism on my M60 was loose and needed replacement. For the time being, I taped it down with green tape. The troops called the green tape,"100 mile an hour tape," as it could virtually hold anything.

I was awarded the prestigious Combat Infantryman Badge (CIB) along with forty-six other soldiers in Alpha Company. We were told about the award, but didn't see the actual documentation until much later. As best I can remember, First Sergeant Cabrera told us we had been awarded the CIB. I think the award was given for Infantry soldiers with more than 90 days assigned to a combat unit who had participated in combat operations. I knew at the time that we met the criteria as we had been there long enough and for sure had seen more than our fair share of action. The order was dated 9 July 1969. I must take this opportunity to list the names of my comrades on the same orders as me:

SGT Joseph Cox
SGT Joseph Simon
SGT Harold Gararbrant
SP5 Charles Kilgore
SP4 Phillip Beck
SP4 Edward Lewis
Sp4 Douglas Beed
SP4 Richard Miller
SP4 Roy Bohn
SP4 Cary Dawkins
SP4 Pete Elsos
SP4 Johnny Norton
SP4 Wayne Sperry
SP4 Jerry Allen
SP4 Harold Carnahan
SP4 James Gray
SP4 Michael Humlicek
SP4 Richard Lovejoy
SP4 Ronald Overton
SP4 David Poulson
PFC Bob Childers

PFC Dewayne Ellrich
PFC Bob Faubert
PFC Roger Johnson
PFC David Rayles
PFC Glenn Schuster
PFC Bob White
PFC Stephen Gray
PFC Edward Anderson
PFC Mark Armantrout
PFC Donnie Canty
PFC Joseph Dillard
PFC Bruce Ellis
PFC Charles Gunn
PFC Raymond Hamill
PFC John Hawkins
PFC Vernon Ikehara
PFC Phillip Jennings
PFC Dennis Klemmer
PFC Isaac Maldonado
PFC Virgil Massey
PFC Daniel McGee
PFC James Mitchell
PFC Louis Ramos
PFC Lovett Williams
PVT Artemio Munoz
PFC Joseph Fair

I am most grateful and honored to be listed on the same orders as these fine men.

Sutton and Strickland were always jabbing at me about using up so much M60 ammo. If we were going into a LZ, I was firing into the wood line from the chopper along with the Door Gunner and Crew Chief. If we made contact with the enemy, I didn't hesitate to "light up" the area. If we blew an ambush, I sprayed the kill zone with lots of ammo. The only drawback was cleaning the weapon after so much firing and the ringing in my ears. I used a lot of ammo in Vietnam. I always figured that was what is was for and if it kept "Charlie" down and not shooting back it was well worth it.

They called me "John Wayne" from time to time. Today, Roger Johnson tells me that he recalled having to grab my shirttail and hold me back, as I would get all geared up and want to go charging ahead. I was not gung ho, nor a hero. I would just get all wired up and the adrenaline would flow. Today, Roger and I stay in contact with each other. It is a blessing.

About this time, we started operating what we called "Eagle Flights." These were daytime aerial assaults by choppers into suspected enemy locations. These were typically platoon operations. Each soldier carried only his weapon, ammunition, grenades, water and one C-ration meal. We traveled very light. The choppers would pick us up at the base camp or firebase. We would fly around for a while, and then swoop down into an open area for landing. The landing zone would not be hit with artillery or mortars, as we wanted to surprise the enemy. We would jump off the chopper and head into the wood line. It is frightful to run into a wood line from an open area. You just didn't know if the enemy was in there or not. Then we would patrol the area for a short period of time hoping to make contact with the enemy.

If no contact was made, it was back to another open area for pick up. Then we would do it all over again. We would make several eagle flights in a day's time. We could cover a huge area in our AO, if you consider all three platoons were doing this. It was nerve racking to go into a landing zone that had not been prepped with artillery or mortars. Even the chopper Pilots and crew didn't like this method very much. We were sitting ducks if we landed in a LZ where the gooks were dug in and waiting for us.

Several times during my time in the bush a Chaplain would visit with us. He would hold church service right there in the jungle. This happened on resupply days when the Company set up a defensive position. The service was non-denominational so all who wanted could attend. I attempted to always attend the service. I sure felt I needed to, and I knew that prayers were answered.

None of us used earplugs and the loud noise from the M16 rifles, M60 machine guns and hand grenades sure affected our hearing. I still recall how my ears would ring for days after firing our weapons, especially the M60 machine gun or hearing a grenade explode. We couldn't patrol with earplugs in. We wanted to hear every little sound we could. We just couldn't stop in the middle of a firefight and put earplugs in. Many of us suffered hearing loss. I told our Medics about the ringing in my ears. They understood and sympathized with us, but really couldn't do anything.

The majority of our time was spent in the jungle. When not in the jungle, our second most common place was at a fire support base. Here we would occupy bunkers on the perimeter and send out platoons or squads to patrol or set up ambushes. This gave us some rest time and a time to write letters home. When we were moved to a base camp, we were thrilled. We got to use the PX (Army store), eat great food, take good long showers, see movies, sleep in tents, play games, drink lots of beer and really share some fun time. Never did I use, nor did I see any of our guys use marijuana. It was called Koon Sa in Vietnamese. Beer and sometimes a drink of whiskey were it. The beer we got was mostly Black Label and sometimes Falstaff. To get a Budweiser was a real treat. Every now and then we would get a Vietnamese beer called "Thirty-Three," because it had a 33 on the label. It came in bottles, not cans. We called it "Tiger Piss," as it was not a very good beer. The American beer came in cans and was opened with a can opener. We called the can opener a "church key."

Now, we did party when we were at the base camps and attempt to forget about the jungle, all the fighting, and those we lost. We had some darn good times together that I will never forget. We drank, laughed and shared valuable time together. We became brothers. I have a great photo of Childers, Sutton, Strickland, Houston, Davis and me with a big stack of empty beer cans in front of us. Also, there's a photo of Big Joe Spruill feeding me a beer.

The Platoon got to ride in a Chinook helicopter a few times. The Chinook was a rather large helicopter with two huge rotors. You loaded and unloaded from a ramp at the rear. What an experience! As we loaded and unloaded you could feel the extreme heat from the two engines and the wash from the massive rotors would literally knock you down. I didn't feel comfortable in the Chinook, as it seemed to be much slower taking off and landing than a Huey and it was a much larger target. It was noisy, vibrated a lot, and you were enclosed where you couldn't see out. I did take a photo or two from the ramp area.

At the local club at Dau Tieng, I went in to have a beer. Now, the club was just a tent with a homemade wooden bar and some tables and chairs. I was sitting at the bar when a Chaplain (the rank of Captain) came up and sat down beside me. He said, "Here son, let me buy you a beer."

Now that took me by complete surprise. I'm from a family of Baptists. Here's a man of the cloth and he's buying me a beer. Boy, did I feel strange. We talked a while and he finally had to leave and told me he wished me the very best. I found out that he was Catholic and that it was acceptable in their religion. My mom would have had a fit. My Dad would have thought it funny.

Another tragic event was in the Michelin Rubber Plantation when we unknowingly fired upon some civilians who were in an area they were not supposed to be. We had several days of contact and were all "geared up." We were patrolling the rubber plantation. Someone in the 2nd Squad, led by Pete Elsos from Washington, saw movement and 1st, 3rd and 4th Squads moved up to form a line. We engaged and started shooting at the movement in the rubber. I fired several rounds, as did everyone else. We were then told to cease-fire, as we were firing into women and children.

The Vietnamese interpreter we had with us was standing up with his pistol and shouting back and forth with the civilians. I could hear women and children crying and screaming. Our Medics were moved forward to render assistance. I remember helicopters coming in to help. It was reported that some women and children were killed or wounded.

I didn't attempt to move up to see. I was terrified and shocked. One guy told me that an old man and young boy were killed and that several were wounded. Another guy said an old woman and young girl were killed with several wounded. I heard later that there was some sort of investigation. I never did hear any more. Here is yet another tragedy of war. I never learned much more about this event. But it has stayed with me through all these years.

Sometime later in July, Captain Coker taught us new ways to patrol in the jungle using football plays. He used chart paper and an easel to show us the plays. That was interesting and different. It helped us understand better what we needed to do. I remember a play called the "buttonhook." I just remember the name, not how it went.

The entire Company was patrolling a large area in the Michelin Rubber Plantation. Lima Platoon was in the middle with November Platoon about 300 meters out on our left flank and Mike Platoon about 300 meters out on our right flank. We were told we were approaching a long, narrow opening in the rubber trees and not to cross the opening. We were to hold at the opening, set-up and observe. The opening was along our entire front from left to right, but it was only about 50 meters across. Lima Platoon arrived at the opening and we had our M60 machine guns take up positions on the left and right covering the open area. Sutton, Strickland, and I had the right position.

As we watched our area, we saw movement about 300 meters. All we could make out was just a brief outline of a man running across the narrow opening from one side of the rubber trees to the other side of the rubber trees. We alerted Lieutenant Holtz who had set up the Platoon CP fairly close to our position. Lieutenant Holtz was on the radio making contact with the other Platoons. We waited a few minutes and it was confirmed that we didn't have any troops crossing the open area. All were held up as ordered. When the man ran across the opening again, I fired at him with the M60 machine gun. I must have fired 40-50 rounds.

All of a sudden, there was radio chatter that Mike Platoon's point squad was taking machine gun fire and the tracer rounds were red. Lieutenant Holtz told us to cease firing. I had already heard the radio and knew in all probability we had fired at our own troops. Sutton, Strickland and I just looked at each other and shook our heads. I saw Sutton cross his hands as if he was praying.

He may well have been. It was reported that no one was hit. I sure was thankful for that. Mike Platoon's point squad had some explaining to do as to why they did not hold up at the opening as ordered. Coordination between fighting elements is crucial. That was proven that day. We were just plain lucky.

We had just come out of the bush when John Sutton and I decided to go to the PX for some goodies while most of the Company was taking showers and getting cleaned-up. We wanted to get ahead of the crowd. We had just come out of the bush after about 10 days and we were dirty and a mess. As we were walking the short distance to the PX, the Brigade Sergeant Major pulled alongside us in his ¼ ton (jeep), jumped out and asked what the hell we were doing.

I told him we had just finished a rather long period in the jungle and we were going to the PX.

I remember him telling us, "Like hell you are. Soldiers in my Brigade are not a bunch of rag bags and I'll be damned if you are going looking like that."

About that time our Battalion Commander pulled up in his ¼ ton (jeep) and asked the Sergeant Major if there was a problem. The Sergeant Major started explaining how dirty we were and that we needed to get our act together and do it right now. The Battalion Commander informed the Sergeant Major that we were his. He then talked in a very low voice to the Sergeant Major. The Sergeant Major turned burning red in the face and jumped into his ¼ ton and took off.

I was astounded and didn't know what to say, so I didn't say anything.

The Battalion Commander told John and me to carry-on.

So we went to the PX. Later on, I would meet the Sergeant Major again and he remembered me.

One day, the Platoon had just been picked up from the bush from a long stay in the jungle. As we were flying, I looked down and spotted gooks in an open field. I pointed to Lieutenant Holtz who also saw them. The gooks were heavily camouflaged and were walking, and then they hit the ground. There were ten to fifteen of them. Lieutenant

Holtz called the sighting in and we were then directed to a LZ (Landing Zone) a short distance away and told to search the area and make contact.

We spent an additional two days in the bush. We didn't make contact. All the troops were complaining and really upset about another two days in the bush. I kept my mouth shut and didn't volunteer to tell them that it was me that first spotted the dinks. I don't think Lieutenant Holtz would have seen them if I hadn't pointed them out to him. A few months later, I did tell John Sutton and he just laughed and said, "Boy, way to go Fair."

Many times when we came out of the bush, after an extended period, the rear troops in our Company would set up a barbecue and have steaks, baked potatoes and drinks for everyone. First Sergeant Cabrera would help with the cooking and serving. It was a real nice treat. I sure enjoyed it. I came from Kentucky where we only had country-fried steak (breaded steak cooked in a frying pan). It was only my second time having a grilled steak and I sure enjoyed it and still do today. I didn't know what rare, medium, well, etc. meant. Of course, the guys were giving me a hard time. I remember Chiser asking, "Boy, where have been your whole life?" He even said, "I need to get you to Chicago." Everyone was laughing. These were great times.

An easy duty was providing security while the Engineers swept the road between Dau Tieng and FSB Mahone. It was about 9-10 "klicks" (9,000 – 10,000 meters) between the two. As the Engineers walked down the road using mine sweepers, the Infantry would provide left, right and rear security. I made a point never to walk on the road. There was no sense in me taking a chance that they missed a mine. We would walk to Dau Tieng in the morning, spend the day there relaxing and "shooting the sh-t," and in the afternoon walk back to FSB Mahone. Now that was the good life for an infantryman.

It seemed when people thought about Vietnam they automatically pictured rice paddies; however, our AO (Area of Operations) was mainly jungle, open areas with tall grass and the rubber plantations. There were a few rice paddies close to many of the villages (hamlets) but I don't recall patrolling in areas where we had to walk the dikes of the rice paddies or go sloshing through the paddies. We heard that the rice paddies were perfect places for the gooks to place anti-personnel mines. Also, walking the dikes made you a perfect target for gook snipers.

Chapter Five

August 1969

I was promoted to SP4 E-4 in August 1969. To me, that meant more money. I was still humping the M60. At that time, the 4th Squad (Weapons Squad) consisted of Spruill, Strickland, Sutton, Martin, Lewis and me.

We were setting up a Company position. Marty Vazanna, Lieutenant Jay Holtz, Lieutenant Mike Hart and Staff Sergeant Michael Schellenberger were examining a trail and deciding how to set up our ambushes. Marty was always mindful of his surroundings and kept a vigilant eye on all. All of a sudden, two gooks walked around the bend in the trail. Luckily, Marty saw them first and sprayed them with a burst of fire from his AR15 rifle. Marty killed one. The other ran and got away.

Later, we booby-trapped the dead gook by placing a hand grenade under him with the pin pulled. His body weight kept the lever held down. We anticipated his buddies would come back for him after we left and they would move the body and detonate the grenade, killing more.

We were informed that Major General Milloy was the new 1st Infantry Division Commander. There was a large Change of Command Ceremony held at Di An, but none of the soldiers from Alpha Company got to go. I don't know where Major General Talbott went.

I assumed he was promoted.

I developed a rather large boil on my butt (right between my butt cheeks). I was miserable and couldn't sit down on my butt and was forced to sit on my side. Thanks to our Medics, Doc Taylor and Doc Gayton, for their fine medical attention they provided to me in the jungle. We were in a Company resupply position. I had to lie face down on a poncho while they opened the boil and allowed it to drain. Boy, it hurt like hell, but what a relief it was when it drained. Doc Taylor surprised me when he said they had removed a small sliver of metal from the boil. I kept thinking *how it could have gotten there and laughingly wondered if I was going to be awarded a Purple Heart.* They gave me some antibiotics to take and cream to apply to the sore. After a few days, I had mended quite well. Our medics were superb. Just last year, I found out that Doc Elmo Taylor from Utah became a PA (Physician's Assistant) when he returned home from Vietnam. I just knew he would do well in the medical field.

What happened if we got disoriented and didn't know exactly where we were? Soldiers never used the term lost. We were only temporarily disoriented. (Today, I use the same term with my wife when we are traveling). There were times in the thick jungle where we were not able to walk in a straight line and therefore being somewhat disoriented could happen. We could easily be up to 300 meters from where we thought we were. That was not a good situation if we made contact with the enemy and needed fire support from artillery, mortars or air support from jets or helicopter gunships. We could easily bring all hell down on our own position. If we became disoriented we would have to find prominent landmarks such as mountains, road intersections, or perhaps a bend in a river on our map. Using a compass, we would shoot an azimuth from our location to at least two of these prominent landmarks and determine the back azimuth. On the map, we would determine the back azimuth from both ground coordinates and where the lines met was where we were located. They call this method a map resection. It was easy and very accurate.

One afternoon Joe Spruill, John Sutton and I were setting up our defensive position on a trail. Joe had crawled out to set his Claymore mine. All of a sudden, he comes crawling rapidly back to the position and shouting, "Gooks!" The gook fired several rounds at him and luckily missed. We returned fire, but didn't hit anything. Later, we were laughing at the look on his face and the way such a big guy could low crawl so fast. We decided he could win the Olympics if low crawling was one of the events.

Joe had forgotten to take a M16 rifle with him when he went to set his Claymore. He was a M60 Gunner and would take an Ammo Bearer's M16 while they manned the M60. He was unarmed when the gook spotted him. I don't believe he ever made that mistake again.

It was sad to discover that Joe passed away in 1974 from a brain aneurism. Joe was from LaGrange, Georgia. He told me about his family there and bragged about his father being the Deputy Police Chief. He jokingly said we could raise some hell and not worry too much about it. He insisted that I visit with him after we got home. It is so sad and unfortunate that I didn't get to visit with Joe as we had planned. We get so wrapped up in our daily lives that we many times skip or put off the small, but yet, most important things. I know Joe would understand.

In May 2013 I had the honor of meeting Joe's sister, Jan, and visiting his gravesite. It was an emotional time for me and helped provide closure to this chapter of my life.

All the troops got a real big laugh when they brought us a movie to watch at Dau Tieng. It was the "Green Berets" starring John Wayne. We watched it and to us it was almost a comedy. We did enjoy the free beer that was provided.

Guarding the bridge at Dau Tieng was good, easy duty and we enjoyed the time out of the bush. The mosquitos were really bad since we were right on a river. It was neat getting to throw concussion grenades into the river from time to time. This was to prevent the gooks from slipping up on the bridge under water. We did have to fill sandbags and were always improving the bunkers, but it sure beat the bush. We could get out of the rain and we got one hot meal per day. You would have thought we were living in a luxury hotel by the way we cherished being there.

There was a black soldier who we called the "Preacher." He was in some type of trouble with the Company and Battalion Commanders. His attitude was terrible and he refused to follow orders. I never knew what happened to him. He carried a sign around his neck that had "Preacher" written on it. Some guys just went south on us and ended up in big time trouble. There were not many, but it was shameful what these guys did.

Ed McAdams, a black guy from New York, turned age 21. A few of us helped him celebrate while we were at Dau Tieng. Staff Sergeant Schellenberger, Jeff Mill and I got two fifths of whiskey and surprised Ed with a small birthday celebration. We couldn't drink fast enough from the whiskey bottles, so we poured the whiskey into a large coffee can. After we all were in a drunken state, Staff Sergeant Schellenberger decided I was too young to drink (I was eighteen years old). I grabbed a 2X4 piece of wood and chased him around the Company area. We were both stumbling and falling. It was a good laugh.

The next day we moved to the bush and the four of us had huge hangovers. Staff Sergeant Schellenberger vomited while we were in the chopper flying out to our LZ. At the time, the chopper crew and the guys with Staff Sergeant Schellenberger didn't think it was funny at all. I was so sick that I couldn't eat anything for a couple of days, but I drank a lot of water. Doc Taylor couldn't do much for a hangover. A few days later, we were all laughing about it.

And then there was the day the deuce-and-a-half (2.5 ton truck) driver, sent to pick us up at the airstrip, got a ticket on the road back to our Company area from some over-zealous MP (Military Police). We had just come in from an extended stay in the bush. Can you believe our truck driver got a ticket for speeding in Vietnam? The MP in his ¼ ton had a flashing light. He shot past our truck and motioned for our truck driver to pull over.

All the troops riding in the back were really whooping and hollering at the MP. We were giving him hell. It was a big laugh for us. The MP was not very happy and he was red as hell in the face. He said he was going to write a report and submit it to our Commander. Wow, now that really got us all worried (just kidding). Some of the guys were even offering the MP their name, rank, date of birth and service number, which is what a US prisoner of war was allowed to give to his captors. I felt a little bad for the MP, but his cocky attitude brought it on. Nothing more ever came about this event.

My sister, Chermain, (who is now deceased) and my brother-in-law, Charlie, sent me a huge box of special candy. We were in Dau Tieng for a two-day rest. What made the candy special was that each piece had some type of liquor in it: whiskey, bourbon, cognac, gin, vodka and you name it. John Sutton and I decided we had to get rid of the stuff before we went back to the bush. We took each piece, cut the top off and drank the small shot of liquor in it. Now, you would think that there is no way we could get a buzz from liquor inside candy. Let me tell you, after about 75 small shots of liquor from 75 pieces of candy each, we got a real buzz, but what was worse is how sick we got. I wrote my sister and thanked her and Charlie for the candy and her thinking of me. I didn't mention how we had abused such a fine gift.

First Sergeant Cabrera came and patrolled the jungle with us from time to time. We were in a firefight in the Michelin Rubber Plantation. Three gooks were killed. One was beheaded from an M79 Grenade round. I saw First Sergeant Cabrera pick up the gook's head and toss it back to where the gook was laying and just slapping his hands as if to dust them off. It didn't bother him at all. I think I overheard him mumble, He'll need this," as he tossed the head.

We had a very young Vietnamese Scout with us at the time. His name was Cho Sok and he was a good Vietnamese scout. I wonder what happened to him after all these years. I kept thinking he didn't know what peace meant as he had been fighting since he was twelve years old.

I learned of William Overstreet's death. He and I were good friends at home. We went to school together, enjoyed a few beers, and even chased some women together before he married Rita Robison, a local gal, who I knew quite well. He was drafted and went into the service about 4 months before I did. William was killed by a booby trap in April 1969. I later heard it was a 105 MM artillery shell that had been booby-trapped to go off. William had walked right by it. It had destroyed his body to the extent that his casket could not be opened at his funeral. His family and mine elected not to tell me for a while. They were hoping that time would let me better adjust to being in Vietnam before laying this on me. I was really concerned about William's wife, Rita.

When I got home I did get the chance to talk with William's brother, JB Overstreet. He was the only family member whom the body was shown to. JB told me there wasn't much left of William. I shed tears for William again that day.

I got stung just below my left eye while we were patrolling in the bush outside Dau Tieng. It looked to me like it was a bee, very much like a yellow jacket. It flew directly at me, landed on my face and stung me. There wasn't much time to react. I am allergic to some bee stings. And, boy, did my face, especially my left eye, swell and swell quickly. Within fifteen minutes my left eye was completely closed and my right eye was partially closed. I couldn't even force my left eye open. I was afraid both eyes would be swelled completely closed.

Doc Fisk checked me out and said I needed to get back to the base camp as soon as possible. Luckily for me, we were less than thirty minutes away from our resupply landing zone. I made the walk to the landing zone and was able to partially see out of my right eye. Of course, some of my buddies were already giving me a hard time. "Hey Fair, that's the best you ever looked. Too bad you didn't get stung where it would have been sexually helpful with all that swelling."

I jumped on the chopper and spent two days at Dau Tieng in the Company area on bed rest after receiving Benadryl. That was nice, but boring, and I sure missed the guys. The hot shower and hot meals were great. I sure was ready to join the unit again.

Of course when I joined up with the unit again the guys just had to give me a hard time. They asked if I enjoyed my R&R and wanted to know what the bee looked like so they could get stung. I told them I had spent two days at the local Vietnamese whorehouse and the healing process worked very well.

Sometimes late at night, while we were lying in the jungle, a plane would fly over and there would be a bang and a bright light would flash. This bright light would really light up the area for just a second. This would be done at intervals as the plane flew over. I asked about this and was told the plane was doing aerial photography for making maps. I assumed this was correct. I didn't know any different.

On August 26th, PFC Verlon King from Oklahoma was killed. I recall this event very well. King was killed from a burst of fire from an AK47. He was not in our Platoon. He was standing up next to a trail when a gook popped up from his hiding position and shot him. I believe he died instantly. Some of the guys returned fire, but the gook got away. Just shortly after that, all hell broke loose and we were receiving a lot of fire from positions deep in the bush. A MEDEVAC chopper was sent to pick up Verlon, but it wouldn't land because there was too much ground fire. To suppress all the incoming fire, they put a "Spooky" gunship up over us. "Spooky" was a helicopter gunship loaded with rockets, 40 MM cannon and mini-guns. It really lit up the area!

The next morning when we scoured the site, we found a gook backpack with a bra and panty set made out of orange parachute silk. We also found a Russian's wallet. It was a long, brown leather wallet with a gold star emblazoned on the outside. Whoever opened it up saw there was a picture of a guy and his name, etc., all written in Cyrillic. This was reported immediately and Battalion sent two guys out to pick it up real quick. Staff Sergeant Schellenberger and Jeff Mill carried Verlon King's body to the LZ where he was picked up.

We were really pissed off at the chopper crew, as they wanted to make sure King's body didn't get blood all over their chopper floor. A poncho was placed down first and King's body placed on top of it. I thought, *to hell with these guys! Didn't they have any feelings? What about respect for a comrade who had been killed?* They needed to spend some time in the bush with us. Washing blood out of a chopper was far easier than having to place a dead comrade on board and seeing him flown away. Everyone was again devastated at losing a fellow soldier.

That same night Nugent was wounded in the thigh from an AK47 round. I can still picture Staff Sergeant Schellenberger carrying Nugent "fireman style" and falling. Nugent was worried that Shelly was hurt with the fall. He kept saying, "I'm okay are you?"

Shelly kept saying, "You are the one wounded, not me."

Shelly was a big, strong man and had little trouble packing Nugent. A MEDEVAC chopper was able to land and picked him up.

We were preparing to move to the jungle again after a short one-day stand down at Dau Tieng. The loss of Verlon King was still heavy on everyone's mind and we sure didn't want to move to the jungle again, but it was what we were ordered to do and what we had to do. We didn't have a choice. We were all sitting or lying around waiting for the truck ride to the airstrip. A newer soldier (I can't recall his name) was really complaining, and rather loudly, about having to go back to the jungle after only a one-day rest. He was bitching about this and about that and was really getting under the skin of some of the guys. Staff Sergeant Schellenberger told him to tone it down, but when he had walked away from the Platoon the guy just kept on bitching.

Finally, Joe Spruill evidently had enough, jumped up and asked the guy, "Boy, are you wearing pink panties?"

The young soldier asked Joe, "What do you mean?"

Joe stated, "With all the bitching you are doing you must be a woman in disguise."

Joe started going around from soldier to soldier asking if they were wearing panties. It was comical the way he was going to each troop and asking to see their panties. He asked me and I said, "Hell no I ain't wearing panties. I'm a man."

Remember, none of us wore any underwear.

When he got to another soldier (I believe it was Roy Bohn) well, old Roy just jumped up, pulled his pants down and mooned everyone. He asked Joe, "Does it look like I have panties on?"

Everyone broke out in laughter and the young troop said, "All right, all right. I get it."

This calmed everyone down. It was a good laugh at a tough time. We were all afraid and dreaded the jungle yet again. Deep down I knew where the newer guy was coming from and I felt sympathy for him. I winked at him and told him to hang in there and everything would be just fine. I acted calm and like I was all tough and hardcore. I wasn't.

Joe Fair - 1969

My first look at Vietnam

Lambretta

Big Red One at Di An

Burning human waste

SP4 Baker Holding the Human Skull

A covered bunker

Joe Fair in full jungle gear

PFC Buroin at the Shower

PFC Baxter at the Pisser

A perimeter bunker

A helicopter in the air

SGT Ehlers on patrol

Rock Davis

Catching a quick nap

Jim Wheeler

Earnest Cartwright at Song Be

Joe Fair and a Donut Dolly at Song Be

Dwayne Ellrich

Ernest Freeman

Bob White and LT Zazarro

Roger Johnson

Rain, rain, rain at BN HQ

Jim Ward writing home

Joe Fair on patrol with his M60

SGT Dale Rilling

Joe Fair & Rock Davis

RTO's White, Ward & Childers

View from FSB Pine Ridge

View of the ground after a B52 bomb run

Shelly, Childers, Taylor, Johnson, Fair & Elsos

SSG Mike Schellenberger (Shelly)

SGT Gary Nugent

Roger Johnson

Taylor, Lewis, Norton & Elsos

BN HQ at Dau Tieng

Roy Bohm

Honoring our dead

Doc Fisk

The Buttercups

Bob Childers

Lima Platoon

Fair, Elsos, Schellenberger, Childers & Taylor

Berl Martin

Eagle flight patrol

Chinook helicopter

CPT Coker

John Sutton

Marty Vazanna

Doc Gayton

Big Joe Spruill

Sperry, Gumble, Spruill & McAdams

1SG Cabrera

Big Joe Spruill & Little Joe Fair

SSG Schellenberger

Joe Fair's 19th birthday

George Knox & Edsel

Ward Neumer & John Sutton

Huey landing at a PZ

Elsos escorting a prisoner

Huey landing at a LZ

Joe Fair and Two Donut Dollies

Dwayne Ellrich with Vietnamese children

Roy Bohn

Jeff Mill

Jeff Mill reading the Stars & Stripes

LT Mike Hart & Johnny Houston

Jim Ward

Swimmimg pool at Dau Tieng

Resupply chopper

Spotter plane in the air

Cobra gunship

Bob White

Mike Prengel

Joe Fair on leave in Sydney

Pop Sperry & Johnny Houston

CPT Rittenhouse and Jim Ward

Colonel Braim's Huey pilot

Colonel Braim's Jeep

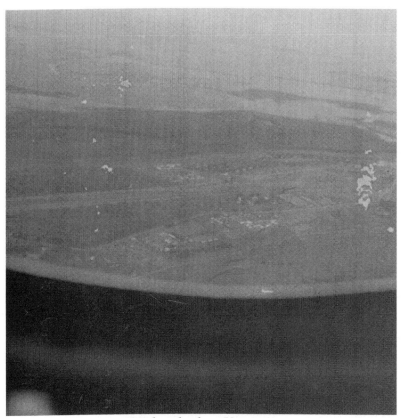

My last look at Vietnam

Chapter Six

September 1969

On September 4th, I turned age 19. We were at Dau Tieng. The guys in my Squad along with some others had pooled their money and purchased a real nice Sanyo radio for me. I have a photo. I didn't want to celebrate by drinking any whiskey as I had definitely learned my lesson when we celebrated Ed McAdams' birthday. We had a few beers, which was plenty for me. It was such a great thing for the guys to do. A special note of thanks to: Schellenberger, Vazanna, Mill, Ward, Childers, Sutton, Strickland, Lewis, Spruill, Johnson, McAdams, Martin, Houston, Chiser, and all those who gave. I was one of the youngest, if not the youngest, in Alpha Company. It seemed that everyone else was 1-5 years older than me.

The rubber harvest in Vietnam is year-round. Since we were right smack dab in the middle of the Michelin Rubber Plantation, we, from time to time, witnessed the Vietnamese people harvesting the raw rubber (natural latex). They had to coordinate with our headquarters to be in the plantation for harvesting. Each rubber tree had a bowl wired to it. A narrow slit was made in the bark of the tree starting about 5-6 feet up the trunk and spiraled around the tree to where the bowl was attached about 3-4 feet from the ground. A pin was driven into the end of the slit. The rubber would ooze from the bark, where it was slit, and run down to the pin then drip into the bowl where it collected. After a while, the liquid rubber would become solid and felt just like a solid rubber ball, not really round, but bowl shaped. The Vietnamese would come along and collect the rubber balls and take them to be processed. Of course—GI's being GI's—we would grab a piece of the solid rubber and throw it at each other. It hurt like hell if it hit you solid. But it was just another thing we all laughed at.

Of course, our leaders kept ordering us to leave the rubber alone.

Joe Spruill was quite a large man. He stood at least 6 feet 5 inches tall. They called him "Big Joe" and me "Little Joe" as we were both carrying M60 machine guns at that time. When we stood together you could see how big he was. I have a photo of us standing together. Not fat, just big. He was a super nice giant.

About this time, we all received a copy of the Black Scarves Annual. It is titled: *1st Battalion, 2nd Infantry Regiment, 1st Infantry Division—Dracula*. This book contained photos of the entire Battalion broken down by the individual soldier, Platoon and Company. Most of the troops were in the book. Some were missed, as they may have been on R&R or in the hospital. It's an excellent piece of the Battalion's history. I believe the photos were taken around late July or early August 1969, as I was still a PFC in the book.

In the "Black Scarves" book is also a photo of Big Joe naked in the shower. We all gave him a hard time as the photo had a heart covering his private parts. We kept kidding him about how small the heart was. The photo was also listed in Bravo Company's section, not Alpha's. We told Joe that he wasn't even noted as being with Alpha Company, as we were ashamed of him. Joe kept telling us we were all just jealous. Troops have a way to help each other maintain sanity. There was always something to laugh and joke about.

I also remember one day we were working with a dog handler and the dog alerted on some gooks. The dog dashed forward toward the gooks. He was shot dead. We had a ceremony for him when we got back to Dau Tieng. I do not recall the dog handler's name or the dog's name. Even though it was for a dog, the ceremony was very moving. That dog gave his life for us.

I do remember George Knox another dog handler with his dog, Edsel. They were a great pair. I couldn't even think about how hard it would be to leave your dog after serving one year together. To me, that would be a difficult part of being a dog handler. The dogs didn't get to go home, and I wondered what became of them. Everyone in the Platoon became friends with George and it was nice to pet and groom Edsel.

Edsel was a great dog, except for the time he pissed on Staff Sergeant Schellenberger's gear that was stacked on the ground. Edsel sniffed the gear, hiked up his leg and took a long piss on the gear. We all got a good laugh, except for Shelly.

When out of the field and at a base camp, we spent a lot of time reading, writing home, drinking beer, and there were several of us that played, or at least attempted to play the guitar. The guitarists I remember were Sergeant Ward Neumer, Doc Fisk, Johnny Houston, Jim Wheeler, Rock Davis, Lieutenant Mike Hart and me. Davis was very talented and could also play the piano. He demonstrated that when we were at Di An for the three day stand down.

I don't recall who owned the two guitars we had. I guess we all did. Boy we sure had some good jam sessions with a lot of singing and yes, even some dancing. I could never move like some of our black guys. Of course, they couldn't clog like us hillbillies. But we sure laughed and had a great time. Chiser said he was a black Fred Astaire.

We performed what they called a "Claymore Extraction" from the field for a Company size extraction. Here's my recollection of how it went and why. In areas known for heavy enemy contact we wanted to ensure we kept the gooks down and not willing to open fire on incoming choppers. The entire Company was set up in a large circular defensive position. We blew the initial Claymore mines just prior to the first wave of choppers touching down. In the first wave, a Platoon along with the Company Command and Control were picked up. The two remaining Platoons formed a closer circle and set up Claymore mines. Once ready, the second wave of choppers was directed to land.

The Company Commander, observing from the air, gave the signal to blow the outer ring just prior to the choppers landing. The Claymores were blown and the choppers landed and picked up the next Platoon. The last Platoon formed a tighter defensive circle and set out their Claymores. Once the Claymore mines were ready, the last wave of choppers was directed to land. The Company

Commander gave the signal to blow the inner ring just prior to the choppers landing. The Claymores were blown, the choppers landed and the last Platoon was picked up. I was part of the last Platoon.

I kept thinking, *the gooks for sure knew where we are at from all these explosions and all the choppers in the air.* This took about 45 minutes. Overall, it didn't make sense to me, and I concluded we were getting rid of old Claymore mines. But I don't believe they had an expiration date on them.

While in the bush, Tommy Gumble from New Jersey, our M79 grenade launcher man, tripped and fell and he accidently fired the M79. I was walking ahead of Gumble. The round just missed me and boy was I pissed off. It scared the hell out of me. The round didn't explode, as it had not traveled far enough to arm itself. Again, it was scary.

Of course Gumble, in his New Jersey way, said, "It don't mean nuffin."

That remark didn't help.

Gumble was a good man, just a whole lot different from us Southerners. Sometimes I struggled to understand what he was saying with his heavy New Jersey accent.

Sometime later that month, I recall Pete Elsos capturing a gook walking down a trail. Pete was a tough soldier and seemed to have no fear. I was astonished by the size of the gook and believed he was Chinese. He was carrying a piece of equipment, but I didn't know what it was. Staff Sergeant Schellenberger thought it was an aiming device for artillery. Pete stepped out on the trail and made the gook surrender. You should have seen the look on his face when Pete popped out onto the trail with his M16 pointed right at him. I was hidden on the other side of the trail and walked out after he threw up his hands. I really didn't do anything. I got some of the credit, but it was all Pete's. We moved to a LZ (Landing Zone) where the prisoner was picked up by a chopper. He was taken to our Headquarters. Later, we heard that he was a significant captive. We didn't know what that meant.

It was important to have an SOP (Standard Operating Procedure) to alert the incoming helicopters where we were in the bush and where to land. The chopper flying overhead would announce to us (via the radio) to "pop smoke." That meant to release a smoke grenade. We would inform the chopper that we had popped smoke and for him to identify the smoke color. He would come back and tell us what color smoke we had popped. If he confirmed the correct color then he would land near the smoke. This kept the gooks from popping a smoke grenade and having the chopper land where they were. The key was not informing the chopper what color we were popping, but have them confirm what color they saw. If it matched what we popped then everything was okay. To the best of my memory, the smoke grenade colors were white, yellow, green and violet. Red was another color, but it was used only to identify enemy positions.

At Dau Tieng the Company had the pleasure of two Donut Dollies visiting with us. I have a photo of me hugging these two charming females and, of course, my wife wants to know the details every time she sees the photo. They spent several hours with us and we played games and had fun.

I vividly remember playing a word game. The group of us was divided into two teams. The girls asked us to come up with words that went with blue, like blue sky. They had an easel with paper on it and were writing the words down. We were all laughing after we had run out of words. The game was tied. Everybody was thinking real hard for another word.

Suddenly, I jumped up and yelled, "Blue bloomers!"

All the guys started laughing.

The girls were also laughing and maybe a little red in the face.

Big Joe gently slapped me on the back of the head and told me to be nice and act like a gentleman. He asked, "Where are you from, Kentucky?"

It was a good laugh for all. My team won the game. Bob Childers took some great photos. It was nice to be around some "round eyes." Their purpose was to help generate positive morale for the troops. It in fact worked. These ladies were a blessing for all the troops they came in contact with. It was like a little taste of home.

Outside of Dau Tieng in the Michelin Rubber Plantation the entire Company was setting up a night defensive position. Ward, Sutton, Strickland and I were sent out about 200 meters to set up an OP (Observation Post). I spotted a gook moving through the wooded area. We were on one hillside and he was on another. There was a hollow between us.

I whispered to Ward, Sutton and Strickland to look, but they said they couldn't spot the gook.

He was slowly and methodically moving from tree to tree trying to maintain concealment.

I got down behind the M60, took aim and fired at the gook. I fired about 100 rounds in six to nine round bursts. I could see him over the barrel of the M60, darting back and forth as I fired, then disappearing. I didn't know if I had hit him or not. We used the radio to assist our FO (Forward Observer) Lieutenant Mike Hart from Minnesota, and his RTO Ron Hume from Texas to call in artillery: a great team that knew what they were doing. I provided adjustments to where the rounds were hitting.

After the artillery barrage, a small group of us went out and searched the area. I had fired up the area as the trees and bush showed. I missed, as we couldn't find the gook. I did get the gook's Ho Chi Minh sandals, as I scared the hell out of him and he ran out of his shoes. That was one lucky fellow. I had a visit with Captain Coker and Lieutenant Holtz back at the CP and had to explain what I saw and how I engaged the enemy. Captain Coker was smiling when I explained using 100 M60 rounds and missing. It was a big joke in the Company. I was slated to attend M60 remedial training (that was part of the big joke on me).

Forty years later, I learned that SSG Michael Schellenberger had fired a round at this guy. He fired one round, missed and his weapon jammed. He smiled when he told me about this. All these years and I thought I was the only one that had spotted and shot at the gook. So, there were two of us that missed.

Charles Strickland (we called him Fuzz) wrote in my 1st Infantry Division Volume II book, "To the worst gunner in the Company, missing a gook 75 times." John Sutton had written, "To the best gunner in the Division." I thought

John's note was more accurate. At least, I liked it far better.

About two weeks later I had my redemption. The 1st Platoon was setting up a night defensive position. I was setting up my M60 position with Sutton and Strickland. Staff Sergeant Schellenberger was in charge of the Platoon as Lieutenant Holtz was on R&R. I was looking out from our position to determine our firing lanes when I spotted a gook moving in the open field about 200 meters from our position. He was walking down an old, overgrown paved road wearing black pants and an olive green shirt. He was not wearing a helmet or any type hat.

I whispered, "gook" and grabbed Staff Sergeant Schellenberger's M16, took careful aim and fired a 3-round burst; I had him lined up perfectly in the sights. I saw the gook fall. I knew I had hit him.

McAdams patted me on the back and said, "You got him Fair."

Staff Sergeant Schellenberger told my Squad to go check it out and the Platoon would provide cover for us.

I grabbed my M60 and Vazanna, Sutton and I went out to search the dead gook. I remember firing my M60 into the area where the gook had fallen. As we came closer, I fired into the gook. Vazanna was firing his M16 as we approached him. We were all scared and wanted to make sure he couldn't fire back. Vazanna and I secured the area while Sutton searched the dead gook. I still vividly recall hearing the moans and groans coming from the dead gook. His body was riddled with bullet holes and a large portion of his head was blown away. I felt for Sutton having to dig through the gook's pockets and gear. I kept thinking, how could he still be alive? Sutton found that he was carrying three 82 MM mortar rounds. They were wrapped in a homemade bamboo carrier. He also had a small knife, but a round had damaged it.

While we were searching the gook, we came under fire from up the trail. Another party of gooks opened up on us with small arms fire. We could hear the crack then pop of the rounds. Vazanna, Sutton and I hit the ground, and returned fire. I fired over 300 M60 rounds and Staff Sergeant Schellenberger from his position called in

Artillery. The gooks broke contact with us. We moved back to our Platoon position.

I got my pride back that day. Staff Sergeant Schellenberger told me, "good job."

I was so proud at that time that I had personally taken out an enemy soldier. The guys were all giving me praises. Big Joe told me, "Way to go little buddy." Fuzz Strickland and Sutton told me, "It's about time with all the ammunition you have used up."

I learned later that very few soldiers had confirmed "kills" in Vietnam. I joined the "elite" along with Marty Vazanna. We had confirmed kills. Later on Captain Coker and Lieutenant Holtz said I didn't have to attend any remedial training. First Sergeant Cabrera made me feel good saying, "Good job Fair, but you wasted too much ammo." I remember he didn't give out much praise.

Then, I was so proud, but now and then I think about that Vietnamese man that I killed and I wonder about his family. I think about him especially during the holidays when my family gathers at home. This event remains vividly clear in my mind even today after all these years.

Chapter Seven

October 1969

The wet season was over and the weather was better, but it was still hot. It was a relief not being wet except from our own sweat. There was plenty of that. Lying down at night in the bush was much better, as we were not lying in water. Oh, but then came the termites. As we lay on the ground on our ponchos, our body heat would bring the termites to the surface where they would commence to chew on the ponchos. They would not bite you, but you could hear them all nightlong munching on the poncho. After several nights of this, they would render the poncho useless, as it would be full of tiny holes. You could hold the poncho up to the sunlight and see all the holes.

It was during this month that, First Sergeant Cabrera informed me that I had received the Air Medal Award. I didn't, at the time, know what it was for. All I could say was thanks. There was no ceremony, so I figured it couldn't mean a whole lot. Later on, I did get a copy of the award orders. There were seven Alpha Company guys on the award:

> SP4 Dwayne Ellrich
> SP4 Cary Dawkins
> SP4 Pete Elsos
> SP4 Bob Faubert
> SP4 Lonnie Gaston
> PFC William Bedwell
> SP4 Joseph Fair

The order stated that it was for meritorious achievement while participating in aerial flight against a hostile force for the period 18 April 1969 to 2 September 1969. I knew we had many, many combat assault missions via the Huey Helicopter. I was honored being listed with all these fine men.

Around this time, I had heard about the city of Vung Tao, which was located on the South Chine Sea in South Vietnam. It was a very popular R&R resort for US combat troops. This is where troops got to go to enjoy two to three days of fun in the sun and the use of China Beach. China Beach, I am told, was an absolutely beautiful beach. Years later, there was an American TV show called "China Beach" that told about doctors and nurses during the Vietnam War. I recall watching this show in the late 80's and early 90's. How a soldier was selected for this in-country R&R was a mystery to me, and many others in our unit. I don't recall any of us ever going on an in-country R&R. Of course curiosity was killing me, so I asked First Sergeant Cabrera about going to Vung Tau for an in-country rest and relaxation period. I told him I thought I deserved it and would really enjoy it. He told me to get it out of my mind and forget about it because I wasn't going. I took his word on it and sure enough I didn't get to go. I still wonder about the selection process.

One image stands out in my mind from the bush. We were in a fairly intense firefight. The green tracers were coming at us. I looked up and First Sergeant Cabrera was standing up. He was standing next to a small sapling holding on to his AR15 rifle. There was no way that little sapling provided him any protection. I motioned for him to get down. I was really concerned about him. He smiled and pointed at me to keep firing. Top was invincible and wasn't going to get dirty for anyone, especially a gook.

Here's a funny thing that happened. Roy Bohn was standing up in full field gear with a rucksack leaning up against a small sapling. He was tired and huffing. The sapling gave way and he fell backwards, feet stuck straight up in the air. He just lay there. What a laugh we all had.

Alex Sole from Philadelphia, Pennsylvania spent two days in the jungle with the inseam of one leg of his pants ripped wide open. The best I remember, he had picked up a pair of pants that had been tailored for a real nice, tight fit rather than the baggy look of the typical Army pant. Many of the rear troops enjoyed this look. The tight fit didn't last very long in the bush and ripped right out. Now remember, we didn't wear any underwear, and there was Alex with all his "stuff" exposed. We were all giving him a hard time. Alex came back at us with, "You guys are all just jealous that you don't have a python of love like me." Luckily for Alex, we received a resupply chopper the third day in the bush and he got new pants.

There was a guy in Mike Platoon who injured his back while we were in the Michelin Rubber Plantation. I don't know how he was injured. It was so bad that the poor guy couldn't even straighten up. He was bent at the waist at a 90-degree angle. All his equipment was removed, including his helmet and M16. Then he had to walk to a LZ to get picked up by a MEDEVAC chopper. He kind of crawled into the chopper. I really felt for the guy, as it was a long walk. He never returned to the unit. Rumor had it that some of the guys saw him later at the Dau Tieng swimming pool doing high dives and flips off the diving board. If that were true, so much for a bad back.

I recall Jeff Mill from Connecticut, getting a wound to his upper thigh (the back side) from a grenade. It wasn't serious, but it stuck in my mind. We were blowing a gook bunker in the jungle. Jeff threw his grenade, but missed the bunker opening. He turned to run, but didn't get far enough. The grenade exploded. I can still see Jeff grabbing the backside of his leg and grimacing. I think he was even a little embarrassed. He had to be air lifted out to the hospital at Dau Tieng, but soon returned to the unit. Jeff was very smart and became an excellent RTO (Radio/Telephone Operator).

If we were blowing a bunker, we were trained to pull the pin on the grenade, count off 3 seconds, and throw the grenade. If the enemy was in the bunker it didn't allow him time to pick up the grenade and throw it back. Sounds good, right? Let me tell you, I knew of no one who wanted to hold that grenade for 3 seconds after the pin was pulled. As soon as we pulled the pin we got rid of that sucker!

Jim Ward was an RTO (Radio/Telephone Operator) in the Platoon. He was from Dayton, Ohio, and really a super nice guy. Jim was having a problem with the shoulder straps on his rucksack rubbing his shoulders raw and causing blistering. Now just imagine carrying a full rucksack, then adding a PRC-25 radio and humping the bush. It was a load. Jim toughed it out and I assume his shoulders became callused and the sores and blisters went away. Jim did not complain. He was a darn good soldier, an excellent RTO and my friend. Later on, he became the RTO for the Company Commander. You had to be an excellent RTO to be assigned to the Company Commander.

Can you believe we lost a guy in the jungle? No, I don't mean killed, but lost. I can't recall his name, but I remember him very well. He was fair skinned, had light, curly hair and wore glasses. We were patrolling outside of FSB Mahone. Our Company had two files of men as we slowly patrolled in heavy bush. The last man of each file was rear security. His job was to maintain a watch over where we had just traveled to make sure the gooks didn't slip up on us from the rear. We stopped for a rest period. Evidently, he fell asleep. When we moved out again he didn't go with us. The closest guy to him had failed to let him know we were moving out. After we had traveled through the bush for about two hours, the report came up from our rear security that a guy was missing. We had walked off and left him. We turned around and went back, but couldn't find him after about two hours. It became dark so we set up our NDP. This poor guy was all on our minds. I can't imagine what he was going through.

Around noon the next day, as we continued to patrol, we received word via the radio that our man had walked into FSB Mahone. He had told them he had spent the night in the bush by himself. He said that he was watching the back trail and when he turned to look up the trail everyone was gone. He had walked a few hundred meters to try to catch up, but the trail we had made in the bush had forked and he didn't know which way to go. It was getting dark so he hunkered down right off the trail and spent the night. The next morning he stayed off the trail, but followed it back to the road that led to FSB Mahone and made his way back. That was one lucky soldier. I don't believe any disciplinary action was taken. To me, his night alone in the bush was enough.

Another mishap occurred one day when Captain Coker went flying with a friend, who was an Australian pilot with a call sign Slugger 1-5, in a RECON plane. The Company was on a two-day rest. The plane was either shot down or had engine failure and they bailed out into the jungle. We were very concerned about him and we were all ready to go to the bush and get him. Later, we heard they were safely airlifted out. Soon after, Captain Coker told us about his adventure. He did state that he was very scared. I would have been also.

At the time, I had recently purchased a real nice, fairly expensive camera at the PX. It was an Olympus Penn F 35mm camera. Of course, I didn't have a clue how to use it and I knew I couldn't take it to the bush. It was too large and cumbersome. I managed to take some rather nice photos of the guys with it after some of the guys helped me with all the fancy settings. I stored it in a locked duffel bag in our rear Company area. One day when we came out of the bush, I discovered my duffel bag had been broken into and the camera was gone. Yes, I was pissed off, but what could I do? I had far greater things on my mind than the loss of a camera.

It was frightening the day we were at our Company area in Dau Tieng preparing to move to the jungle. We had just come off a two-day rest and were loading up on ammunition, water and C-rations. We were burning our trash in 55-gallon drums as we tore away the wood, cardboard and paper from the ammunition crates and C-ration boxes. All of a sudden, one of the burning trashcans exploded and sent shrapnel and burning embers in all directions. There were a few guys who were wounded. Luckily there were no serious injuries. This caused one hell of a disruption to our operational plan that day. We were delayed several hours as the wounded were taken care of and we were on hold. The follow-up investigation indicated that a hand grenade had accidentally been tossed into one of the burning drums along with a bunch of paper and cardboard.

One good thing about Dau Tieng was the swimming pool. This pool was part of the French Plantation Quarters. Not only could you cool off and enjoy the fellowship and swimming, it was great for skin rashes such as ringworm. The pool was chlorinated very strongly just for this purpose. You could feel the skin burning where you had a rash, but soon that went away. Our Medics insisted we get into the pool if we had a skin rash. We didn't have swimming trunks or shorts but cut-off fatigue pants worked very well. Some of the rear-echelon troops didn't like to see us grunts come to the pool, especially the ones with real bad rashes. There was not much they could do about it as we came in numbers and we sure had each other's back. Mess with one and you messed with all.

Mike Prengel from Illinois was one great swimmer and boy could he dive. I was afraid to dive off the board, but managed enough courage to jump. I made it to the end of the diving board, but I chickened out. Then I got pushed off the board. That was my one and only time coming off that diving board. Everyone around the pool was heckling me, but I didn't mind. I could take the heckling better than getting on that diving board again.

Dau Tieng also had a small snack bar that was located close to the swimming pool. It was very nice and you could get a soft drink, hamburger and fries. Located with the snack bar was a shop where you could get items packaged and sent home. I did manage to send my mom two Vietnamese hand paintings. They were very nice. I still have them today.

How did we keep our hair cut? We had a Vietnamese Barber who had an air-conditioned trailer parked at Dau Tieng. It was a modern barbershop. When we came out of the bush, for a rest period, we all made sure we got a trim. I believe it cost one dollar in MPC. There were a few times we trimmed each other's hair with scissors and shaved the neck with a razor but that always turned out pretty bad. Each base camp had a Vietnamese barbershop.

The Bob Hope Show visited the 1st Infantry troops at Lai Khe. I don't know how the Army determined who got to go, but none of the guys in our Company went. I assume since we were now headquartered out of Dau Tieng and not Lai Khe, it didn't make sense for the Army to transport us there. We did hear and read about what a great show it was, featuring actress-singer Connie Stevens, Teresa

Graves and the "Golddiggers." The guys were all complaining that they hoped the rear-echelon troops enjoyed the show as the Infantry had to stay in the bush and protect their asses. That was typical expressions by the Infantry guys.

The Vietnamese children were precious. Just like all little children they were curious and asked a lot of questions. It was amazing how much of the English language they knew. The children were also teaching us Vietnamese words. We would point at an object, say it in English, and the children would say it in Vietnamese. We heard stories of the children blowing themselves up along with American soldiers. Never did we see this. From time to time, we would have to run the kids off, as they would gather around us in small groups. We felt we were placing them in danger. "Di Di Mau" was Vietnamese to move quickly or go away. "Lai Dai" meant come here.

The Vietnamese people were fascinating to watch, especially the children and old folks. We were in a defensive position just a short distance from FSB Mahone. We were providing observation on the road between Dau Tieng and FSB Mahone. About 20 meters from my position, an old man was using a small bucket to remove water from an old bomb crater off the side of the road. He would dip the bucket full from the crater then pour the water into the ditch along the side of the road. I watched and wondered why he was doing this.

After working for about an hour he had the water level in the crater down to about six inches or a less. He stopped dipping and then I realized he was catching frogs and large tadpoles from the crater by hand. As he caught the small frogs, he would break their backs and throw them into his bucket. Of course they couldn't jump out with a broken back. He looked up at me and smiled and said, "Chop-Chop."

I just smiled. I thought of home and all the good, abundant food we readily had at our tables. I felt sad for the old man. If most Americans only knew what he, and others, went through, here in Vietnam, just to have a meal.

Later on that month, Lima Platoon had set up an ambush on an old paved road. The Company CP had set up with us. My position was just in front of the CP so I heard everything going on. Three gooks were spotted standing at an intersection down the road about 200 to 300 meters from our position. Lieutenant Mike Hart called in an artillery mission on the gooks. The rounds came in and hit right on the gooks. There must have been 5-6 rounds. There was no adjustment of fire. All three gooks were hit. Two were killed and one was seriously injured. Our Medic was called forward and rendered first aid. Later, a MEDEVAC was called in and the wounded gook was air lifted to the hospital in Dau Tieng.

Lieutenant Hart was bragging about his accuracy of calling in the artillery fire mission. Captain Coker was jokingly giving him a hard time and told him that, "With a paved road and the gooks standing at an intersection it was nearly impossible to miss." A paved road intersection was a precise known map point. It would be easy to call a fire mission on such a target. Like I had mentioned before, when we made a kill we left them lying where they were killed.

The US Army had propaganda units. Part of their efforts was to drop leaflets in the jungle to hopefully entice the Viet Cong to surrender by offering them amnesty. Many times while on patrol we would find these leaflets. This was called the Chieu Hoi or "open arms" program. Any Viet Cong who took this offer of amnesty was called a Chieu Hoi. There were several times that we had a Chieu Hoi working with us. It was difficult for us to place much trust in them. Just think, one day the enemy, the next day our friend. It just didn't work well. We spent too much effort keeping an eye on them rather than our mission.

I was helping unload a resupply chopper in an LZ outside of Dau Tieng. We were in a hurry to get the chopper unloaded so it could move from the area. As I grabbed a wooden box of M60 ammunition (about 100 pounds) and pulled it from the chopper, it slipped and fell on my toes on both feet. It hit the hardest on my right big toe and man did it hurt. It took my breath. I was jumping up and down and grimacing badly. The chopper took off. The guys helping me were looking at me wondering what the thunder I was doing. I finally caught my breath and sat down and removed my right sock and boot. I told the guys what I had done. My right big toe sure was red. Doc Gayton looked at it, said it wasn't broken and that I should be all right. He stated that I might lose my toenail. It hurt like hell for a few days, I took plenty of aspirin and soon the pain subsided. Since the pain had gone away, I didn't pay much attention to my toe except when I would pull my boots off and sprinkle my feet with foot powder. I could see the toenail was very discolored.

Chapter Eight

November 1969

Finally, after five months, I got to hand the M60 machine gun over to a newer troop. I believe it was PFC Greenwood. I became the 4th Squad Leader as an E-4. I helped Greenwood in his new role. I knew what it was like to be given the heavy firepower of the Platoon. It was a huge responsibility. I just knew he would do well. I knew his first few weeks would be very hard until he adjusted to carrying the M60. I showed him a few "tricks of the trade" and helped him as best I could.

I was now an experienced leader who young guys looked up to. Sergeant Davis, (not the Davis from Minnesota who had already left for the world) and I were in charge of a Squad ambush. Sergeant Davis, who was fairly new to the Platoon, was a "Shake and Bake" NCO, but he proved himself quite rapidly to the troops and me. That night, around midnight, there was a lot of noise on the trail. We were scared to death, as was the entire Squad. We listened intently and kept hearing what we thought were whispers and movement. It was right on the trail in front of our position. We alerted the rest of the Squad. Everyone was on edge. We made the decision and blew our Claymores and fired our small arms. We saturated the trail in front of us with fire. Then we moved back to a defensive position away from the trail.

It was an intense period waiting for daylight. At daybreak, Davis and I slowly moved out to the trail as the others in the Squad provided security. We checked the trail and found we had killed two wild pigs. We sure were hesitant to call it in on the radio to the CP for we knew it would bring a lot of laughter and mockery from the whole Company. Well, it sure did that. Even the guys in our Squad were laughing. Davis and I got some good ribbing from the other Squads and Platoons. We were okay with it and knew we would eventually get back at them. Every now and then someone would oink or grunt at us, which started the laughter. What's that old saying? "What comes around goes around." We just knew we would eventually get even. It was truly comical. I can still laugh about it today.

The two pigs were the only wild animals I saw in the jungle. I had heard many stories about elephants, tigers, monkeys and snakes, but during my entire tour I did not see any during all the time we patrolled the jungle. I am still amazed that we didn't see any snakes considering all the time we laid on the ground. I have quite a fear of snakes, but I have to tell you they didn't even cross my mind when we were patrolling and laying in ambush for the enemy.

I had a tooth filled at Dau Tieng by the Division Dental Officer. The tooth was giving me some pain from time to time and when we were on a two-day rest I saw the dentist. It only showed a small cavity on the outside, but when it was drilled the cavity was quite large. It was strange as the tooth was filled with a pink, plastic looking filling. The dentist told me it was a temporary filling and that when I got back stateside I needed to have it filled permanently. When I did get stateside, the army dentist at Ft. Meade, MD pulled the tooth. He said it should have been permanently filled in Vietnam. Oh well.

I was able to adjust artillery fire on a target via our FO (Forward Observer) who was an Artillery officer assigned to our unit. Lieutenant Hart and his RTO Ron Hume were still assigned to our Company. We were just outside the Michelin Rubber Plantation and in fairly thick vegetation. We made contact with the enemy. Our Squad and another Squad were laying down fire with our M16's and the M60 machine guns. The return fire was intense and the FO called in Artillery. From my position, which was way forward of the FO, I was able to call back to him via our RTO the adjustments to bring the artillery rounds right on top of the enemy positions. From the initial round, the adjustments were in meters; left or right or add or drop. Once the adjustment round was on top of the target, then it was "fire for effect" and several rounds came in on the target. We called this bringing smoke on the target. Boy, could the Artillery bring havoc on the enemy and their defenses. We swept the area after contact was broken. There was quite a bit of blood, but no dinks were found. They had carried off their dead or wounded. This happened many, many times.

We also had air support from helicopters, fixed wing planes and jets. I will never forget the 300 or 500 pound bombs dropped by the jets. What an explosion they made, and the damage was unbelievable! There was a time that it was dropped "danger close" to our position. We were taking a lot of fire and it was determined to drop the rounds real close so that we would not be overtaken by the gooks. Seeing those jets come in at high speed, drop their bombs and then pull away was really something. The noise as they pulled away was earth shattering. The ground shook and dirt, leaves and debris were thrown everywhere when the bombs exploded. You could actually feel the concussion from the bombs. Contact with the gooks was broken.

Then there was the napalm. Napalm is like jellied gasoline. It is an extreme anti-personnel weapon. The fireball from a napalm round was something to witness. No one could live through a direct hit. Several times we watched as napalm was dropped on enemy positions. Gooks burned up in the fireballs were called "crispy critters." It sounds awful, but this was just another way soldiers dealt with the horror of war to maintain some sanity. It was common to hear over the radio, "We have crispy critters." To see a human body that had been completely burned was shocking. It didn't even look human.

We had made fairly heavy contact with the enemy and we were following a small group of gooks through the bush in hot pursuit. We had suffered no casualties, but knew we had inflicted some suffering on them as we had saturated the area with heavy fire from our M16's and M60's. We came upon a small clearing and found, under a tree, some very bloody bandages. It was evident they had stopped and were rendering aid to their comrades. We continued to follow and from time to time we would spot the blood trail.

My senses were on super alert. We kept thinking we would be ambushed. It's hair raising to be in pursuit rather than lying in ambush and waiting for the enemy to come to you. We continued the pursuit a while longer, but finally gave up on it. We had lost all sign of the gooks. A report was made to our headquarters.

We had a female Viet Cong prisoner who joined our Company along with a Vietnamese Interpreter. She was going to lead us to a huge bunker complex in the Iron Triangle. We spent two or three nights in the jungle with her, but nothing developed from all the patrolling. I kept thinking about how small she was and she was the enemy. I just couldn't find myself afraid of her.

From time to time, the Battalion Support Company would provide a sniper to the Infantry Line companies. A M14 Rifle Sniper was assigned to our Platoon. He flew out to us on a resupply chopper. He had just finished the 1st Infantry Division's Sniper School. I can't recall his name but he told me he had been "in country" about two months, but this was his first assignment to an Infantry Line Company. We were setting up our NDP (Night Defensive Position) and I watched him get out his rubber air mattress and start blowing it up. I hated to break the news to him, but we didn't use air mattresses in the bush. They made far too much noise when you were laying on them and turned over. They were also just too much additional weight to carry. I said to him, "We don't use air mattresses."

He replied, "You've got to be kidding." Then he asked, "Am I supposed to sleep directly on the ground?"

I told him that we slept on a poncho and poncho liner. They worked quite well.

I helped him get rid of some gear that he didn't need and had him trash his drawers and T–shirt. He remained with us a few days. This reminded me of the first day I joined the unit way back in April. I sure felt for him.

The one story I will share, which still mystifies me is the day, is of when I was setting up my Claymore mine on a trail. We were outside of Dau Tieng and there was a Vietnamese cemetery to our immediate front, with a trail running between the cemetery and us. Sutton and

Strickland were digging the fighting position. I had moved out to the trail to set up my Claymore mine. I had lain my M16 down beside me and was placing the detonator into the mine. Low and behold, I looked up and there was a gook, standing on the trail about 5 meters away, looking at me. He was fully equipped and was carrying an AK47. I dove down and reached for my M16. When I looked up, he was gone. Why he didn't shoot is beyond me. I believe he was an NVA, as he was in full khaki uniform. Perhaps I was so terrified, and I was, that he really wasn't looking directly at me. I just thought he was. I can still see that image today. That was a close call for me.

Late one night, a Cobra gunship was flying above us. It hovered directly above us and commenced firing its minigun. Every fifth round was a red tracer, but when it fired it fired so rapidly it was a single, continuous red line that came from the gunship and touched the ground. It didn't sound like a weapon firing, as it was a long burrrrrrrrr each time it fired. The links from the gun belt were falling from the sky all around us as the gunship fired. It was a sight to see (and hear) the firing so close. Imagine 2,000 rounds per minute hitting the target!

Thanksgiving Day came and was gone and we didn't even notice. We were in the jungle doing our routine patrolling and setting up ambushes. Some of the guys were asking, "Is it Thanksgiving?" I thought about it a few days later. I hoped my family was doing well.

I recall a major firefight we were involved in when Joe Spruill was awarded the Bronze Star with a "V" device for heroism. We were on an ambush patrol outside a village. Two VC were seen at the edge of the village. At the same time, we were informed that a larger group of VC was escaping from the rear of the village and running to the wood line. We were moving to block the VC when we came under intense small arms and machine gun fire from another group. Big Joe grabbed his M60 machine gun and, along with his machine gun crew, moved forward in the line of fire. Joe managed to place a devastating volume of fire on the VC that wounded several and forced them to retreat.

It takes a brave man to move forward when you are under heavy fire. Big Joe didn't flinch, as he knew he was taking care of his comrades. His official award of the Bronze Star with "V" device for valor was made on December 18, 1969. It was a moving ceremony as we watched Big Joe and others being honored. I sure was proud of him and the others. Joe told the 4th Squad and me that he didn't know why he was getting an award. We convinced him he deserved it. I felt he and the others deserved even more.

The PX at Dau Tieng was running a special for new cars. I couldn't believe you could buy a car while in Vietnam. I assume they were doing this all over Vietnam. I hope I recall correctly. If you had less than three months left on your tour, you could pre-order a new car. Ford, GM and Chrysler were making special deals for GI's. I heard that they could arrange for the car to be waiting for you at your hometown when you got home. I remember the muscle cars were the "in" thing. The Ford Mustang, Chevy Camaro, Pontiac GTO, Oldsmobile 442, Dodge Charger, and Plymouth GTX are some I recall. I knew of a couple guys who purchased a vehicle through this sales promotion. I didn't think I wanted to take part in this. I kept asking myself, "What happens if I get killed?" Who gets the car and the balance of the payments? Lord knows I didn't want to put this added burden on my parents. It just wasn't for me. It was really strange seeing such deals made from a combat zone. I didn't think I could afford a new car anyway.

Chapter Nine

December 1969

I was promoted to Sergeant E-5 early December 1969. Some of the guys (especially Sutton, Strickland and Spruill) were giving me a hard time saying I had kissed enough butt and I should get it and if I kept on I'd make General. I took the ribbing with good stride. The guys asked me if I was now the boss and had to tell them what to do. They wanted to know what would happen if they didn't follow my orders. I told them they had to do exactly what I said and to think of me as the "Big Cheese" or the "Head Honcho." Not following my orders meant facing a firing squad. Fuzz Strickland reminded me of my poor shooting abilities. He just had to bring up firing 100 M60 rounds and missing a gook.

The US Army was introducing the M203, a new weapon. It was an M16 rifle with a grenade launcher underneath the M16 barrel. It was two weapons rolled into one: the M16 rifle and the M79 grenade launcher. We all got to go outside Dau Tieng and fire the new weapon. It was pretty neat and it sure seemed to fit well into the Army's arsenal. The guys really liked it. There was a drawback; not only did the guy assigned the M203 have to carry his full load of M16 ammo (20 magazines with 18 rounds each) but he had to carry the 40MM rounds (10-15 rounds) for the launcher. More weight to hump in the bush. I believe it was four to eight guys per Platoon who were assigned the new M203.

On December 3rd SP4 Mike Prengel was killed accidently on the flight line at Dau Tieng by his friend. I recall this tragedy quite well. We were there waiting to be airlifted out to the bush. We were all lying around, talking, reading and some sleeping. I have sympathy for his friend who has lived with this tragedy. I vividly remember the sound of the M16 rifle going off. I quickly looked up and saw Mike fall backwards and hit the tarmac. He was probably 10-15 feet from me. I remember his friend yelling, "No, no, no!" and bending over Mike. The Medics and Platoon Leader ran to Mike's aid. I saw Mike's eyes fluttering and then he lost his body control and starting peeing straight up in the air. They must have pulled his pants down while rendering him aid and trying to determine where he was hit. His eyes glazed over and I just knew he was gone.

A Major from Battalion came running around to all of us and telling us to clear (unload) our weapons. He was shouting and furious. I can see why. As the choppers came in to pick us up we all reloaded (locked and loaded) our weapons and, rightfully so, as we were going to the jungle again. As the choppers lifted off, we all could see them loading Mike into an ambulance.

Later, I learned that Mike and his buddy were goofing off with their M16's and while they were pointed at each other one was fired accidentally. Mike's death was noted as an accidental homicide. What a tragedy. I have a mental photo of Mike that is very clear even today after all these years. He was a darn good guy.

I went on R&R to Sydney Australia in Mid-December. I had Mom send me $600. Now that was a lot of money in 1969. Typically, R&R was taken as close to the middle of the tour as possible. I had waited almost nine months in order to get to go to Sydney. It was one of the first choices for R&R. Other places I could have asked for were Hong Kong, Bangkok, Taipei, Manila, and Singapore. I wanted to go to a place more like home. Married guys got to go to Hawaii to meet their wives.

I hitched a chopper ride from Dau Tieng to Lai Khe. From Lai Khe, I flew in a small fixed wing plane called a C7A Caribou to Di An. From there, it was a bus ride to Tan Son Nhut airbase for the flight to Sydney. I met Ted Baxter, a guy from Bravo Company, who was also going on R&R to Sydney. We traveled together and spent a lot of time together in Sydney. I never saw Ted again after we had returned to Dau Tieng.

At the airport in Sydney, there was a special military clothing store where you could buy or rent civilian clothing. I didn't have any so I spent several dollars on purchasing clothes. Can you believe it, but I didn't have any underwear: no drawers or T-shirts. I did rent a sports jacket just in case I needed one. I had a great time and enjoyed being back to civilization.

I stayed at the Aztar Hotel on Bondi Beach. My first bath took me a couple of hours. While bathing, I looked down and noticed how black my right big toe nail was. I pulled at the nail and it came off. Underneath the black nail was a new, fully-grown nail. Several weeks ago I had dropped an ammo box on my foot. It hurt like hell, but I just let it go. I chuckled at myself.

I remember waking up my first morning (at least, I thought it was morning) and I did not know where I was. I looked around the room and it didn't register in my mind for quite some time where I was. It scared me. I finally figured it out. I looked at the clock and it was 6 o'clock. I called room service and asked for breakfast. They said it would take some doing, but thought they could put together some eggs and bacon. I asked what the problem was and the lady told me it was 6 o'clock PM. I had slept 22 hours straight my first night! I jumped up, and thought, *I am missing out on all the good times. I've got to get going!*

I called Mom and Dad from the hotel. It was great talking to them. I spent some time on the beach, which was nice but hot. It was December, which is summer in Australia. I enjoyed the cool, air-conditioned rooms much more.

I spent a lot of time downtown Sydney at the King's Crossing area. That's where most of the nightclubs were located and most of the single girls. If my memory is correct, there were three real popular clubs: the Whiskey A Go-Go, the Toy Tiger and Texas Down Under. It was a short taxi ride to and from the hotel to the clubs. Hey, they drove on the wrong side of the road. For a country boy, that was something to see. I was riding in what looked like a Chevrolet, but it was called a Holden. The local Sydney guys got me started drinking the local beer called Victoria Bitter. It was very good. The Aussies are darn good people. I had a great time, but spent too much money. I returned to Vietnam with less than $100.

So it was back to the bush again. I dreaded getting hot, dirty, and sleeping on the ground. Most of all I dreaded being back in a combat zone. But I was most thankful to be with the guys again. They kept hounding me to tell them all about Sydney. I exaggerated and told them about all the beer I drank and all the women I had been with. They wanted to know the details, especially about the women. I told them it was just too much for me to bring up those pleasant memories and I'd only add to their torture and mine.

The Company CP (Command Post) had set up with our Platoon about an hour before dark at an NDP (Night Defensive Position). The CP was just a few meters from my position. I could hear Captain Coker, the Company Commander, talking to a Squad Leader. I don't recall which Squad. The Squad was setting up an ambush and had forgotten to take their regular RTO with them and did not know what the new radio frequency was going to be after midnight. The radio frequencies changed each day after midnight. The new frequency couldn't just be given over the radio in the clear for fear the gooks would be monitoring the airways and pick up the frequency. The new frequency was 60.90. I got a big laugh out of Captain Coker who informed the Squad Leader to use the good old American inverted love position and just add two zeros. Well, we all knew he meant 69. The Squad Leader figured it out quickly as he replied, "gotcha" and at midnight changed the frequency to 60.90. At midnight, he reported all was well. Captain Coker was a fast thinker.

Another time November Platoon was leading the Company march. We came in contact and a firefight developed. It was a short contact, as they broke and ran. November Platoon dug up five gook bodies from a grave. They had been there a few days and the stench was awful. We concluded these bodies were the results of a firefight we had had several days ago.

We were in a base camp with lots of booby traps, and Pop Sperry and Jeff Mill went off to scout out some bunkers. Sperry found an ammo can buried in the ground and when he pulled the can up it blew up. He received injuries to both eyes, which blinded him and he couldn't hear too well. They took him out with a jungle penetrator. The penetrator was lowered from a hovering chopper down into the jungle. We had some real small "newbie" ride up with him to balance it. I never heard how Sperry fared, but I sure wished him the very best.

The "Ballad of the Green Berets" was a song written by Staff Sergeant Barry Sadler in 1966. It was played many, many times by the Armed Forces Radio Station in Vietnam. Johnny Houston and I thought we should have a song about the Big Red One, our unit, the 1st Infantry Division. We worked all day on the song while we were on a two-day rest at Dau Tieng. We took the "Ballad of the Green Berets" and changed the words. We used the same key. As best I can remember, here is what we came up with:

"The Ballad of the Big Red One"

Fighting soldiers on the ground
Fearless men who hump around
Men who do what's to be done
Courage lives in the Big Red One

Trained to fight in Charlie's land
Trained to fight, even hand to hand
Trained to do what's to be done
The brave men of the Big Red One

Back at home his loved one waits
Her man has died and met his fate
He has died for those oppressed
Leaving her this last request

Please let my son in the infantry
Oh, let him become an 11B
Let him do what's to be done
He'll be part of the Big Red One

Yes courage lives in the Big Red One
We're all proud of the Big Red One

There may have been another verse, but I can't recall it. This was a darn good hit with our guys as Johnny and I sang and played it. There were even a few tears.

On Christmas Day, 1969, we were in the bush and it was just another day to us. We were outside Dau Tieng in the Michelin Rubber Plantation again patrolling and setting up ambushes. We heard there was supposed to be a ceasefire during Christmas, but to us it really didn't go into effect. We didn't change our tactics and I don't think the gooks did either. It sure didn't seem like Christmas and to us it wasn't. I wondered about my family and friends and hoped all was well. That was my first Christmas away from home. It was a very moving time for all of us. Later on, we did get a hot turkey meal sent to the bush. It was darn good.

Captain Rittenhouse assumed command of Alpha Company. Captain Coker was an absolutely superb commander. I sure respected him greatly and still do today.

I found out the officers generally served in a command for six months. Enlisted soldiers generally served twelve months. The Sergeant Majors and First Sergeants did the best they could at pulling the Enlisted soldiers out of the bush after 9-10 months. They would typically place them in supply or as drivers. Some Enlisted stayed in the bush their entire one-year tour.

Staff Sergeant Schellenberger (Shelly) and I received the Army Commendation Medal for our service in Vietnam. The order was dated 26 December 1969. There were sixteen soldiers listed receiving the award. We were the only 1st Battalion 2nd Infantry soldiers on the orders. Shelly's was for the period of 9 July 1969 to 11 October 1969. Mine was for the period 3 September 1969 to 26 November 1969. We didn't know we had received an award until much later when we were provided a copy of the orders. There was no ceremony. I wondered what I had done to get an award. I assumed just being there was enough to get the award.

Chapter Ten

January 1970

Lieutenant Colonel Anson assumed command of the Battalion. I always felt that Lieutenant Colonel Holt was a good commander and he sure had my respect. I met Lieutenant Colonel Anson, but didn't get the opportunity to work under him for very long.

First Sergeant Cabrera and others had determined that I had done enough time in the bush so in mid-January 1970 I was assigned to Battalion then moved to Brigade working for Colonel Braim, the 1ˢᵗ Brigade Commander. The Brigade Headquarters was at Lai Khe.

By this time, many of my comrades were in the process or had already left Vietnam. Vazanna, Davis, Wheeler, Johnson, Bohn, Childers, Ellrich, Elsos, and Cartwright were just a few who had already left. It was a very tough and emotional time for me, as I had to say good-bye to many of my fellow soldiers who I had served with over the past 10 months: Staff Sergeant Schellenberger, Taylor, Spruill, Sutton, Strickland, Lewis, Chiser, Hume, Martin, Baxter, Mill, Ward, Houston, Neumer, and McAdams. There were others. These guys told me I needed to go. I had done my time on the line. I had more time in country and in the bush than them.

I wanted to get out of the bush, but I also wanted to stay with my comrades. It was a really tough time for me. I felt guilty. Sutton told me, "Joe, it's your time to move on. You can't stay and you shouldn't stay. Hell, we are all looking for the day we get to leave the bush. You have done more than your part. You have seen some of the worst times the unit has gone through." I sure wanted them to go with me. But it just couldn't be that way. I shook each one's hands, gave them a hug and wished them the very best. I sure was proud of those guys. I turned and left. I didn't want the guys to see my tears and there were lots of them. Later on in life, I learned that it's okay for a man to cry. I had already cried far too many times. I didn't see any of the guys again.

My stay at the Battalion Headquarters was very short. Perhaps 5-7 days at the most. I was the driver for the S-1 Officer. I can't recall his name. It seems I didn't fit in well with them so they put my name in for the 1ˢᵗ Brigade. It looked like they sure wanted to get rid of me and fast. I never could figure out why I was not accepted at the Battalion. Perhaps they wanted to get me to Brigade, as I was such an outstanding soldier, really smart and good-looking.

No, that couldn't have been it.

How it was determined that I was qualified to work for a Colonel, is beyond me. I had to meet with Colonel Paul Braim in order to be selected as his Driver and Aid. It seemed he just liked me because he asked very few questions. I remember telling him that I had never been an RTO (Radio Telephone Operator) and knew very little about a PRC25 (Radio). I told him I had walked point, carried the M60 for six months and was the Weapons Squad Leader for about three months. I told him I was good at reading a map, setting up an ambush and operating in the jungle. He asked if I had seen any action and I told him I had seen my fair share. That seemed to be all he wanted to know.

I met the Brigade Sergeant Major and already I could tell he didn't like me. He, I believe, remembered me from our previous engagement with my Battalion Commander and I believe it was also due to the Colonel not asking the Sergeant Major for his input on the selection for the Driver and Assistant to the Brigade Commander. I recall the Sergeant Major telling me to keep my sh-t together or else. I didn't know what the else would be other than return to the bush. I just smiled at him. My big smile angered him and he walked off shaking his head.

One thing I really hated to give up was wearing my black scarf. I took my scarf, folded it up and stored it in my duffel bag. It sure meant a lot to me. I knew that from henceforth the 1ˢᵗ Battalion "Black Scarves," Call Sign "Dracula" would always be a part of me. Never would I forget. How could I? What a bunch we were.

I was provided a desk to work from. Hell, I didn't have any paperwork and I was seldom ever there! I did manage to write a few letters home from my desk. I also started my "Short-timer" calendar. Any soldier with less than 100 days was considered a "short-timer." Most of the troops, in the rear area, had a calendar that they marked off the days as they went by. I soon just threw mine away. I felt sorry for the troops who still had a long time to go. It seemed to me that a short-timer calendar just made them feel worse. I didn't brag about how few days I had left in Vietnam but I sure was anxious to go home.

My sleeping quarter was in a large plantation house. These plantation homes that the US Army occupied were absolutely beautiful. Many were two and three story stucco style houses with tile roofs, large front and back porches. The one I was quartered in had a beautiful spiral staircase. It looked like it was made of real expensive wood. I assumed it was mahogany. My quarters were in the kitchen and pantry, which of course were not being used. It was a nice area. I didn't get to see much of it except late at night getting to bed and early in the morning getting out of bed. It sure beat the bush and sleeping on the ground.

Colonel Braim was a super busy commander and worked from daylight to dark every day. He was always on the go. I thought, for his age, he had a ton of energy. He wanted to be where the action was. Colonel Braim's quarters were a mobile home. It was just like being home. From time to time, the Colonel would have me check on his quarters and ensure the Vietnamese Maid was taking care of his laundry and housekeeping correctly. I had to admit it; there were times I stayed and drank a beer or two from his refrigerator. He always had Bud. Sitting in the cool, air-conditioned mobile home, listening to the radio and having a cold one was just great. I think he knew I had done this a few times.

The accidental shooting investigation of Mike Prengel was still going on. I was surprised. I said a few words to the soldier who accidently shot him. He was at the Brigade Headquarters waiting to see Colonel Braim. It seems he was an E-5 Sergeant. I can't recall his name. It seemed it was Reilly. If my memory serves me correctly, he was of medium height, stocky build and wore glasses. I really felt sorry for him. His eyes and voice relayed how distraught he was over accidentally killing his best friend. I was told last year that when he was transferred back to the states in early 1970 he had skipped to Canada to avoid court-martial and possible time in prison. This may be just a rumor. I still feel sorry for him even today. I can't imagine what he has gone through.

A unit had captured a high-ranking NVA officer and he was being held at the Brigade Headquarters. Someone told me he was a Colonel in the North Vietnamese Army. I had the opportunity to guard him, along with some MP's, for a few hours. I didn't talk to him. I just watched him. You could tell he was an officer by the way he carried himself. He sure didn't look like he could harm anyone, but I knew better.

I saw Bob White at the Brigade TOC (Tactical Operation Center). He was a good RTO (Radio Telephone Operator) in Alpha Company. He had been transferred to Brigade a few weeks before me. I knew he would do well in the TOC. He was from Chattanooga, TN.

After Vietnam, Bob and I were stationed at Ft. Meade, MD together. He spent a night with my parents and me on the farm in June 1970. We drove to Ft. Meade together from Kentucky. Bob was the map-reader while we drove to Maryland. When we were approaching a bridge over a river, he would act as if was holding a PRC 25 radio mic in his hand and state, "Dracula One-Three, this is Charlie Mike Five-Four. Approaching blue line and will cross in fifteen seconds. Charlie Mike Five-Four out." We would laugh and shake our heads. My wife and I visited with his wife and him while at Ft. Meade. They were just darn good people and our friends. I've lost touch with Bob over the years.

I was very concerned about Alpha Company, my old unit. I worried about the guys. I wondered how the guys were doing. Every chance I got, I would check with Bob at the TOC and see if there was any news about them. When I would see Bob he would sometimes say to me, "Black Scarves Call Sign Dracula." He was also proud of his time with Alpha Company. I checked the casualty reports and looked for any from Alpha Company. Fortunately there were no KIA's (Killed in Action).

We were told that the 1st Infantry Division was being pulled out of Vietnam and being deployed back to Ft. Riley, Kansas. We were told that it would be sometime in April. We didn't hear the exact date. Of course this news got a lot of guys really excited, especially the guys who were still fairly new and had a lot of time left on their tour. My time was up in March, so it wasn't going to affect me. We didn't have any details on how the deployment was going to be made and for now it didn't have any effect on what we were doing. We were all told to continue our missions.

The Army should have waited and made the announcement much, much closer to the actual deployment date. Far too many guys had this on their mind rather than doing their job, especially the guys still in the bush.

Chapter Eleven

February 1970

Being with Colonel Braim was really something. I guess I was looking for the easy life, out of the jungle and no fighting. Well, I had to spend nights in the jungle as Colonel Braim enjoyed being with the troops. I recall spending a night with a platoon from the 2nd Battalion 16th Infantry. They were a bunch of good guys. One of their new guys made a comment about my clean uniform. Colonel Braim and I had just landed and joined up with the unit. I just smiled at him. If he only knew what I had seen and done the last 11 months I was sure he would be thinking differently. They blew an ambush and the next day Colonel Braim wanted to see the results. There were four dead gooks lying on an old road. Their bodies were riddled by the Claymore mines, M60 and M16 rounds. Here I was back in the bush and looking at dead gooks. I thought perhaps the war might never end for me. It seemed I just couldn't get away from it.

What got to me were the numerous times we flew in his helicopter over the areas where firefights were taking place. The Colonel loved being on the spot just above the fighting to have firsthand knowledge of what was going on. He even carried an ammo can full of hand grenades that he loved to drop into the jungle. I kept thinking that we were sitting ducks. Every now and then we would see green traces coming up toward us. I kept thinking *it's safer in the bush than up here*. The Pilots were good at keeping the chopper moving and preventing us from being a still target. I made friends with the Pilots and the Crew Chief and Door Gunner. They were another group of good guys. The Crew Chief's last name was Freeman. I thought of Earnest Freeman when I first met him. There was no relationship. These guys made up one damn good helicopter crew.

I struggled with operating the radio. I had previously mentioned I never carried it and used it very little when I was in the bush. I relied on our RTO's. I had not been taught how to use the classified codebook that provided the daily call signs, radio frequencies, and coding/decoding charts.

One time in the field, I was carrying the PRC25. We were with an Infantry Company. Colonel Braim was well ahead of me walking with the Infantry Company Commander. I was told to provide our position (coordinates) to our chopper that was coming in to pick us up. I told a Captain from Brigade Headquarters, who was with us, that I didn't know how to convert the coordinates into the code. He grabbed the handset from me and, using the codebook, called in the coded coordinates.

He glared at me and said, "You are not worthy of being called a Combat Sergeant." He asked, "How the hell did you get to be the Colonel's Driver?"

He was a Staff Officer, didn't have the (CIB) Combat Infantryman Badge, and had little if any experience in an Infantry Line Company. He did this in front of other troops we were with. At the time, I was so mad, I could have shot that son-of-a bitch right on the spot, but I just took the ass chewing and went on. I have to tell you that was the maddest I can ever recall being. I didn't mention it to Colonel Braim. It was my problem and I would handle it.

Later on, I took it upon myself and had one of the Lieutenants in the TOC to explain the codebook and how it worked. It was fairly easy after I was taught. Unfortunately, I didn't get the opportunity to use it. Oh, how I wanted to prove to that Captain I could.

A couple of times, we took the Colonel's chopper and fly to Di An or Long Binh to pick up supplies for the Colonel. We flew quite high, out of harm's way, and listen to the Armed Forces Vietnam Radio station. They played all the hits of the time. Some of the songs I remember were, "I Can't Get No Satisfaction," "Walk a Mile in My Shoes," "We Gotta Get Out of This Place," " Sitting On The Dock of the Bay," "Silver Wings," and "Ballad of the Green Berets." There were many others. Up there we were in another world. It was a real nice trip getting away from it all just for a few hours.

One day we were loading up on the Colonel's chopper. There wasn't enough room left for me to get on board. The Colonel, sitting on the chopper, looked around and pointed at a Major and told him to get off. Then, he pointed at me and said, "Get on." I got a real glaring stare from the Major as he got off the chopper, but what could I do? I climbed on board. I think the Colonel enjoyed my company more than the officers and preferred me riding with him on his chopper as I didn't ask questions, kept my mouth shut, did what I was told to do and didn't attempt to suck up to him.

Two days later, I was driving the Colonel in his ¼ ton with the Major, from the chopper incident, and the Brigade Sergeant Major in the back seat. These two did not like me. We were on a major highway. I came to a stop sign. I stopped, looked both ways then moved on. The Major informed me, after the Colonel departed the jeep, that I needed to improve my driving skills, as I hadn't come to a full stop at the intersection. Any more infractions and I was done. I didn't know what done meant, but I just smiled, shook my head and shrugged it off. The Major was steaming when I was just smiling back at him.

Can you believe it, but I ran into this same Major at Fort Meade, MD. When he saw me he said to me, "I see you made it. Here, state side, it's a different story and you will know who is in charge."

I saluted with a big smile and said, "Yes sir."

My salute was half-ass.

He turned deep red in the face and walked off. I think the big smile did him in again. Luckily, I was being discharged from the Army in a few days and I didn't see him again. I sure wanted to punch his lights out.

I was driving Colonel Braim from a Vietnamese Colonel's headquarters back to our Brigade Headquarters. The Colonel had had a few drinks. He told me about dining with the Vietnamese. He liked their liquor, but hated the food. I was surprised when he told me that he was getting older and didn't know if he would make a general officer or not. I could tell he aspired to make the rank of Brigadier General. I remember telling him that I thought he was a damn good leader and if he wasn't promoted to General the Army was darn right foolish. I told him that I was certain he would soon be promoted. He thanked me for my thoughts. I'll never forget when he told me I was a damn good young man.

Colonel Braim was invited to observe a South Vietnamese Army award ceremony being held at Lai Khe. I watched the ceremony from the Colonel's jeep. I was quite moved by the ceremony as the South Vietnamese Colonel (I think that was his rank) awarded medals to several South Vietnamese soldiers for bravery. Later, Colonel Braim told me the medals were much the same as the American Bronze Star medal with "V" device for valor. Colonel Braim told to me that the ARVN's (Army of the Republic of Vietnam –the South Vietnamese Army) was far better than what they were portrayed to be by the media and by many US Army units. He mentioned they had a very high casualty rate and fought damn hard for their country. Later, I read that there were 1,394,000 South Vietnamese Army casualties (killed and wounded). They had given much for their country. I never had the opportunity to work with any of the ARVN units.

Chapter Twelve

March 1970

More information came down from Headquarters regarding the redeployment of the 1st Infantry Division back to Fort Riley, Kansas. At first, it sounded like the whole Division was going to be pulled out. Later on, we found out that any soldier who had less than two months remaining on their one-year tour would be redeployed. Everyone else would be transferred to other units.

That went over like a turd in a lunch box. Soldiers, who had been in country with the 1st Division for up to 10 months, were going to be placed in other units like the 9th Infantry Division, 101st Airborne, 1st Cavalry, 25th Infantry, etc. Not that these were bad units, but it was like starting all over again. Meeting new guys and learning how the unit operated was a real challenge. I really felt bad for these guys. Later on, I found out that Martin went to the 1st Cavalry, Mill and Ward went to the 9th Infantry and LaSante went to the 101st Airborne. Staff Sergeant Schellenberger came home a month early.

I was awarded, along with several other men of the brigade, the Bronze Star medal for meritorious achievement in ground operations against hostile forces for the period of 15 December 1969 to 15 March 1970. I didn't know many of the other recipients. It was a very nice awards ceremony and I sure appreciated Colonel Braim pinning the Bronze Star on my shirt pocket flap. He said to me, "You're a fine young man and a damn good soldier." I replied, "Thank you sir." I was proud and all smiles.

Later, when I got home, the Army had mailed to my home two more awards: the Army Commendation Medal with Oak Leaf Cluster for meritorious service in Vietnam for the period April 1969 to April 1970 and also the Bronze Star Medal with Oak Leaf Cluster for meritorious achievement in ground operations against hostile forces in

Vietnam for the period of April 1969 to April 1970. I was glad to get the medals, but they didn't mean as much since there was no presentation ceremony. It seemed to me that it degraded the awards to just get them in the mail.

I was provided orders to return to the states in mid-March. At last, my DEROS (Date Eligible for Return from Overseas) had come. I said good-bye to Colonel Braim and wished him the best. It was a tough, emotional thing to do. Again, he told me I was a good soldier and he wished me the best. That was a good compliment from a good career soldier. Again, I shed another tear. He was a good man and a good leader. He was a tough old bastard that I looked up to. Just within the past year, I did find out that Colonel Paul Braim retired as a Colonel. He didn't make the rank of Brigadier General. He was a Professor Emeritus of Embry Riddle Aeronautical University. He died at his home in Pennsylvania on August 25, 2001. He was one hell of a soldier and leader. I had the utmost respect for him.

I traveled from Lai Khe to Di An by deuce-and-a-half in a convoy. There I was traveling back down Highway 13; the way I had come twelve months ago. I was riding shotgun in the front seat. Two guys were on the back manning an M60 machine gun. I thought, *now is not the time to be ambushed*. Thankfully, it was an uneventful ride in the convoy.

At Di An, I was told to report to Supply. There I turned in my M16 and all my field gear. I hesitated to give up my weapon, as I was so accustomed to having a weapon with me at all times. I felt naked without it. All I had were a few items of clothing, a shaving kit and some odds and ends items in a duffel bag. The duffel bag was less than half full. I left Vietnam with less than I had when I got there. I was told I would be issued new military clothing stateside.

I then reported to the S-1 (Personnel Building). I was informed by a clerk that I had to process out. I didn't know what that meant. I asked him, "How do I do that?"

He said, "Look man you're an NCO, so figure it out."

I just took the papers outside, sat down on the steps and initialed different initials on the form for all the places I was to have checked off. It took me less than five minutes and I walked back into the office and handed the form to the clerk. It worked, as he told me I was cleared and good to go.

I was given a brochure: *Tour 365*. It was for soldiers going home. I threw it in my duffel bag. I didn't read it until years later. When I did read it, I found that it was very interesting and most important it said "thank you." It is another one of my small Vietnam War treasures.

I then traveled from Di An to Long Binh or Bien Hoa by bus. I can't remember. I exchanged my MPC for US currency. I think I had around $20. Then it was on to Tan Son Nut Air Base by bus. Here they examined all my belongings to ensure I wasn't taking anything illegal home. I assumed they were looking for a weapon and other illegal contraband.

An Air Force NCO was calling out our names and we lined up to board the plane. It sure was moving to hear my name announced. I was going home. I saw new soldiers in their spanking new uniforms just getting to Vietnam. I really felt compassion for them. There I was, deeply tanned and my uniform was well worn. I had dug out my Black Scarf and proudly wore it around my neck. I was the only troop there wearing a Black Scarf. As I passed by them, all lined up, I nodded my head at them and gave them a smile and a thumbs up. There was no way that I could ridicule them in any manner. Now I was an experienced combat veteran. I had completed my tour. I had earned the CIB (Combat Infantryman Badge). I wondered if they respected me like I had done those I saw leaving Vietnam one year ago. Then I boarded the plane for the flight to the US. All flights home were called "freedom birds." Walking up those steps to enter the plane was something else. I looked back over my shoulder at my last look at Vietnam. I just can't describe it. I was going home.

I took my seat and as I sat there thoughts were racing through my mind. As the plane lifted off the runway, there were cheers throughout the plane by all the soldiers. I even cheered. I looked out the window and as we flew away from the airport I thought, to myself, how fortunate I had been to not only make it but to have served with some of the greatest men one could ever meet. I thought of the soldiers who had left before me and wondered how they were doing.

I thought of the soldiers still in Vietnam and wondered where they were at that moment and hoping all were well. I thought, *why am I leaving and they must stay?* I felt guilty. Then I thought of those who didn't make it. I pondered about their families and how they must feel. They gave "all" that I might have a future and the opportunity to make the best of my life.

I committed to them right there and then to do my best and make a future that they could be proud of. I promised to be a good man. I promised to not be a complainer. I promised to be content and happy. With my wife, family and my life thus far, I hope I have lived up to what I felt were their expectations and my commitments. I hoped one day we would meet again.

A soldier sitting next to me asked, "Hey man, what's the deal with the black scarf?"

Epilogue

We landed at Travis Air Force in the morning after about a sixteen-hour flight from Vietnam. What a thrill it was to hit American soil! I just couldn't believe I was back in America. It's indescribable, the feeling I had. We were taken by bus to Oakland Army Terminal where we were fed a great eggs and steak meal for breakfast. We received our brand new Class A (dress green) uniform and all our medals, badges and insignias and I took a long hot shower and got into my uniform. Boy, did I feel weird. We were issued our airline tickets to the closest airport to our home. Mine was to Louisville, KY. A couple guys and I took a taxi to the San Francisco Airport rather than wait for the Army bus. We were all geared up and anxious to get home.

I had a three-hour delay before my flight to Louisville so I decided I would have a beer and chill out for a bit. I walked up to the bar and ordered a beer. The bartender asked to see my identification, which I thought was strange since I was in uniform. But I proudly showed him my military I.D. card and watched as he looked it over carefully. He then informed me that I was not age twenty-one and he could not serve me alcohol. I replied, "You have got to be kidding me."

He replied, "I'm sorry young man, but the law is the law."

I just moved to the back of the bar and grabbed a table and waited for my boarding time. I had been buying and drinking beer for the past twelve months. I was old enough and mature enough to fight my country's wars, but too young and too immature to purchase and drink an alcoholic beverage. I was angry, disappointed and confused.

An older gentleman came to my table and sat a beer in front of me. He said, "Son, this one is on me. Thank you for your service."

I replied, "Thank you sir, but you don't have to do this. You might get in trouble."

He said, "It's the least I can do."

Well, I drank that beer and noticed the bartender looking at me, but he just let it go.

There were no parades and honoring of the soldiers returning from Vietnam. Each soldier had his own homecoming. My family and friends sure helped me celebrate my return. I was so thankful that I had made it home, alive and all in one piece. I had heard stories of soldiers being harassed and ridiculed by the general public while traveling in uniform. I was told some soldiers changed into civilian clothes while traveling to help prevent the harassment. Fortunately, I never had to endure this.

My thirty-day leave was well spent at home resting, relaxing, seeing and being with my family and friends. I bought a real nice 1964 Chevrolet Impala and spent lots of hours cleaning, polishing, and really making it look sharp. I just knew I could pick up chicks with my good looks and a great looking car. (Okay, with the great looking car). I had tons of time on my hands.

I started dating Regnia Gail (Ginny Gail) Gabehart, who I had known for a long time and who later became my wife. (Many Southern gals are called by use of both their first and middle names). I couldn't believe it when I asked her out and she accepted, as she was good looking, had a nice figure and there were a lot of guys after her. Now forty-three years later, I am still one lucky and fortunate guy.

It was a slow process adjusting to being home and around people other than my fellow soldiers. Not being in the jungle and out of harm's way was a strange feeling. I jumped and ducked at loud noises, felt insecure without my M16 rifle, was constantly observing my surroundings (I guess I was still looking for the enemy), and had trouble sleeping at night. I struggled getting used to wearing civilian clothes, especially shoes. I still had not started wearing underwear. I stayed cold all the time. Coming from a tropical jungle to spring in Kentucky was a shock to the body.

Waking up in the morning, after a fretful night, I would just lie there and think about Vietnam and all the guys. I just couldn't get Vietnam and especially the guys off my mind. I prayed all were safe. It seemed as though I had left my family a second time. I had a girlfriend now and I was happy, but still uncertain about it all.

My body rejected my Mom's home cooking and I made several trips to our family physician, Dr. Mann, for severe stomach cramps and diarrhea. He kept telling me that I would soon adjust and, sure enough, after two or three weeks I was much better.

Close to the end of my thirty-day leave, my orders were mailed to me at home and instructed me to report to Ft. Hamilton, NY. I thought, *where in the thunder is Ft. Hamilton, NY and what kind of army post is it?*

I reluctantly left home. It was not as bad as when I was leaving for Vietnam. Mom and Dad were much more relaxed. I hated to leave my new girlfriend, but I knew I would see her in a month or so. I arrived and was in shock. I contemplated going AWOL (Absent With-Out Leave). Fort Hamilton is located in the southwestern corner of New York City in the borough of Brooklyn. It is a very small army post, perhaps sixty acres at the most. At the time the post was, I believe, training chaplains. Now, what in the world was the army thinking when they assign a young country bumpkin from Kentucky, trained and experienced in infantry fighting, to such a place? I was in the "big city" and completely at a loss.

Fortunately, there was a Chaplain (he was a Major) there who immediately saw that I was out of place and my assignment wasn't going to work. I stayed there for only three days.

I was ordered to the Pentagon in Washington, DC for unit assignment changes. I enjoyed visiting Washington and all the monuments. Now, the Pentagon is a building all should visit. I was lost and kept asking for directions to the Personnel Offices. There were many floors and what they called rings on each floor. Finally, I met with a Colonel Harrison, he and the Chaplain at Ft. Hamilton were best friends, which made it possible for me to see him. The Colonel had me re-assigned to Ft. Meade, MD with the 6th

ACR (Armored Cavalry Regiment). He told me that was the best he could do. It seemed he was in a hurry and didn't have a lot of time to spend looking for my next assignment.

Ft Meade was located between Washington, DC and Baltimore, MD. It was far better than Ft. Hamilton, as it was a large post with combat units. There was just a handful of Vietnam Veterans assigned to my troop. Why the US Army didn't assign me to Ft. Knox, KY or Ft. Campbell, KY is beyond me. I couldn't understand why I wasn't assigned to an infantry unit. I guess that's the Army way.

Part of the overall mission of the 6th ACR was riot control for Washington, DC. On May 4, 1970 the Kent Sate Massacre occurred, which led to riots in Washington, DC starting on May 9, 1970. Over 100,000 people marched on Washington and the rioting commenced.

The 6th ACR was called to respond, therefore we moved to Washington, DC in full riot gear (M-14 rifle with bayonet, helmet, gas mask, canteen, and web gear). Riding in the back of a deuce-and-a-half, I kept asking myself why this was happening. I was confused. I had only been back from Vietnam for less than two months, and I was ordered to confront Americans who were breaking the law and causing havoc in the city. I couldn't believe I was doing this. What were these people thinking?

We formed a defensive perimeter around the US Treasury building. We stood at attention, had our M14 rifle with bayonet (it was sheathed) at port-arms (held up in front of our body at the ready), and were in full riot gear. Young people were coming up to us yelling in our faces calling us baby killers, government dogs, warmongers, etc. Some were throwing water, rocks and trash at us.

There was a young lady, wearing a dress, who squatted down, defecated on the ground, then picked it up and flung it at us. I just knew she was high on drugs. She looked like she was out of her mind.

Another young lady came up to a soldier standing right beside me. She lifted her skirt, straddled his leg and pissed all over his leg. He wasn't able to restrain himself and hit her in the chin with his rifle butt. It was called a butt stroke. She went down hard and was unconscious.

Fortunately, two medics were able to get to her, load her on a stretcher and then load her into an ambulance. I knew she was hurt bad. This sure calmed down many of the rioters. I think they were shocked to see what happened.

The Commander pulled the soldier off the line. I don't believe he received any punishment. We never heard how the young lady faired. I stood there mad as hell and feeling my country was letting me down.

Everything seemed so strange to me. Here I was, back in the world (the United States) and I felt out of place, almost lost. I wondered, had I changed that much or had the world changed?

We stayed in Washington, DC for five straight days pulling guard duty around key buildings and bridges. We slept in small tents and ate "C" rations. It was good getting back to Ft. Meade and what I thought would be some sanity.

I was sent to Ft. Knox, KY on temporary assignment for six weeks to attend the US Army's Basic NCO (Non-commissioned Officer) School. First Sergeant Rodriquez tried to help me get as close to home as possible, even if it was for only six weeks. He was also a Vietnam veteran and had been with the "Big Red One," my old unit. Hey, I was sixty miles from home and enjoying being in Kentucky. I drove home two or three times per week. There were only two other Vietnam veterans in the class: one in Supply and the other in Finance. The class was for soldiers who planned on making a career in the Army: not me at the time. I managed to make it through the school (it was all spit and polish) and graduated 115 out of a class of 118. At least I wasn't dead last, but close to it. The school wasn't all that bad; it's just that my heart wasn't in it.

My wife and I were married on July 18, 1970. It was a rather large wedding. My long-time friends, Wendell Rainwater and Roger Hovious, were my two best men. My wife was absolutely stunning and I was in my Army "Dress Greens." My Mom and Dad were proud of me standing there in my uniform. I remember Mom crying happy tears. I still laugh when I recall Wendell and Roger telling me, as we stood alone in a small room at the back of the church waiting for the wedding service to begin, "now would be a good time to run." I told them I was going to see this thing through. Tony Davis, WR Robison, Byron Eastridge, and Roger Pike, other very close friends, were also there. They sure showed their support. I love all these guys like a brother.

My wife and I lived at Ft. Meade until I was discharged from the US Army in June 1971.

Drug abuse was heavy and racial tensions were very high during my time at Ft. Meade. I was not accustomed to being around either. Twice while I was on CQ (Charge of Quarters), I found a black soldier dead from overdose: one lying dead in his bunk, the other dead in the latrine. I heard both had died from an overdose of heroin. In a way, it was like I was back in a combat zone. There I was seeing dead soldiers once again.

My stateside life in the military was hitting me hard like a ton of bricks. I had thoughts about volunteering to go back to Vietnam where I knew I would fit in better, things made much more sense to me, and what would be expected of me would be much clearer. I knew I needed and wanted to stay with my new wife, as going back to Vietnam would have been unfair to her and I didn't want to leave her and place undue hardships on her. I knew things were going to get better.

Finally, I was discharged from the US Army and left Ft. Meade in June 1971. I did meet some mighty fine people at Ft. Meade. As time marched on, my life just kept getting better. It is that way today, even though I am still haunted by the tragic events of Vietnam. Those events, I know, will never leave me.

I had to tell about this part of my Army career, as it showed how complicated and confusing life could be. Coming from a war zone to home and trying to figure it all out was nearly impossible. Fighting in a war, confronting rioting fellow citizens, drug abuse and high racial tension weighed heavily on me. Understanding all that had happened and was happening just would not register in my mind. These were tough times, not only for me personally, but I felt for all Americans. It seemed as if we were all living our lives on different pages. There were so many different opinions, and the negative politics of Vietnam were so prominent. There was no coming together, no common cause. I kept wondering if Vietnam was worth all that we had and were fighting for.

I joined the Kentucky Army National Guard in 1974, as a second career, and had a great, long career totaling 27 years. I served in Desert Shield and Desert Storm from December 1990 to June 1991. Coming home to a hero's welcome was absolutely awesome. I served with some darn good men including my brother, Terry, who was only eleven years old when I was in Vietnam. It was something serving with your brother in a war. I have to tell you that I was really concerned about his safety.

When we came home, there were parades, picnics and lots of speeches by many politicians and local dignitaries. It was really nice, and patriotism was very high. I shook a lot of hands and hugged many good-looking ladies. My wife and children told me how proud they were of me. I was proud to march with my fellow soldiers in our clean, camouflaged battle dress uniforms, but I kept thinking about all the guys I served with in Vietnam. As I marched in formation, I sure wished they could have been there with me: marching, smiling, waving at the crowd and feeling proud and patriotic. I was proud to be an American soldier. I was proud of my country. Today, I stand proud and I am so thankful to be an American.

I dedicate this book to all whom I served with and with a special note of deep, sincere appreciation to those who did not come home. This is from the heart!

Here's a list of our unit's KIA's (Killed in Action) during my tour from April 1969 to March 1970:

LT Alphonso Chaviz—27 May--hot LZ outside of Song Be
PFC Gary Corrie—12 May—ground attack at Quan Loi
PFC David Demings—12 May—ground attack at Quan Loi
SP4 Earnest Freeman—12 May—ground attack at Quan Loi
PFC Donald Garret—12 May—ground attack at Quan Loi
PFC Ronald Gray—12 May—ground attack at Quan Loi
SP4 Verlon King—26 August—firefight outside Dau Tieng
PFC Lawrence Harvey—12 May—ground attack at Quan Loi
SP4 Robert Lewis—12 May—ground attack at Quan Loi
SP4 Raymond Norvell--12 May—ground attack at Quan Loi
SP4 David Peterson—9 May—firefight outside Quan Loi
LT Guy Pratt—9 May—firefight outside Quan Loi

SP4 Michael Prengel—3 December—accidental shooting at Dau Tieng
SP4 Cecil Queen—12 May—ground attack at Quan Loi
SSG Thomas Sizemore—7 July—incoming mortar attack at Mahone
SP4 Kenneth Smith—27 May—hot LZ outside of Song Be
SP4 Charles Stultz—12 May—ground attack at Quan Loi
SP4 Bobby Yewell—12 May—ground attack at Quan Loi

I must also mention William Overstreet again, who was killed in April 1969. He was my hometown friend.

My fellow soldiers and I ate, drank, slept, laughed, cried and fought together. Skin color or where you were from had no place in our hearts and minds. We were brothers, comrades and friends. We had each other's back. We depended upon each other and took care of each other. What a bunch we were. Unless you've been there and done it, you can't understand what we had together.

I have now forgiven the enemy. The NVA and VC were soldiers fighting for a cause they and their country believed in while I fought for the cause I, and my country, believed in.

One can forgive, but one cannot forget.

I have not mentioned anything about the "politics" of the Vietnam War. I left this to the politicians. We had no time or desire to think about politics. The troops I served with and I were called to serve our country. We did so with honor, dignity and the belief that we were doing the right thing. History will determine if the war was justifiable. Many movies have been produced about the Vietnam War. Many portray the US Vietnam soldiers as warmongers, potheads, rapists and undisciplined soldiers. This was far from the truth during my tour and all the soldiers I served with. I am proud of my service and the service of my fellow soldiers.

Thousands of Vietnam Veterans earned medals for bravery every day. A few were even awarded.

Here are important facts that must be remembered about the Vietnam War:
The US lost 58,156
The 1st Infantry Division lost 3,151
The 2nd Infantry Regiment lost 542
The 1st Battalion ("Black Scarves") lost 276

Alpha Company lost 58

If everyone does not come home, none of the rest of us can ever fully come home either. We all left a piece of our soul in Vietnam.

Many soldiers were killed. Many were wounded and carry their visible scars for life. Many carry invisible mental scars for life.

Long live the memories of the Vietnam War and all the sacrifices of so many. Let us never forget those who gave it all.

Glossary
Words and Phrases of the Vietnam War

ACAV: armored cavalry assault vehicle.

A DUFFEL BAG DRAG AND A BOWL OF CORN FLAKES: the final meal at Ton Son Nhut Air Force Base prior to boarding the Big bird for the flight back to the land of the big PX.

AIT: Advanced Individual Training came right after Basic Training.

ALPHA-ALPHA: automatic ambush, a combination of claymore mines configured to detonate simultaneously when triggered by a trip-wire/battery mechanism.

ALPHA BRAVO: slang expression for ambush, taken from the initials AB.

AMF: literally, "Adios, Mother F-----r."

AMMO: ammunition.

A-O: area of operations.

APC: an armored personnel carrier.

ARVN: Army of the Republic of Vietnam (Army of South Vietnam).

B-40 ROCKET: a shoulder-held RPG launcher.

BAC SI: Vietnamese term for Medical Corpsman/Doctor.

BA-MA-BA: was a term for "33" Vietnamese beer ("Tiger Piss").

BANANA CLIP: banana shaped magazine, standard on the AK-47 assault rifle.

BIC (biet): Vietnamese term for "understand."

BIRD: any aircraft, usually helicopters.

BLUE LINE: a river on a map.

BO DOI: a uniformed NVA soldier.

BOHICA: short for "Bend Over, Here It Comes Again." Usually describing another undesirable assignment.

BOK-BOK: fight/fighting.

BOOKOO: (beaucoup) Vietnamese/French term for "many," or "lots of..."

BOOM BOOM: was a "short time" with a prostitute, typically costing $3-$5.

BOONDOCKS, BOONIES, BRUSH, BUSH: expressions for the jungle, or any remote area away from a base camp or city; sometimes used to refer to any area in Vietnam.

BOUNCING BETTY: explosive that propels upward about four feet into the air and then detonates.

BREAK SQUELCH: to send a "click-hiss" signal on a radio by depressing the push-to-talk button without speaking.

BRING SMOKE: to direct intense artillery fire or air force ordnance on an enemy position.

BUTTER BAR: 2nd Lieutenant, based on the insignia —a single gold bar.

C-4: a very stable plastic explosive carried by infantry soldiers.

CA: combat assault.

CACA DAU: Vietnamese Phrase for "I'll kill you."

CAV: nickname for air cavalry. Also referred to armored cavalry using M113 APCs, and other light armored vehicles.

C & C: command and control.

CHARLIE, CHARLES, CHUCK: Vietcong—short for the phonetic representation Victor Charlie.

CHECK IT OUT: slang as ubiquitous as "okay" during the late sixties, meaning to have a close look at something or someone.

CHERRY: a new troop replacement.

CHICKEN PLATE: chest protector (body armor) worn by helicopter gunners.

CHICOM (Cheye-com): a term describing a Chinese Communist or weapons manufactured in China.

CHIEU HOI (Choo Hoy): "Open Arms" a program under which GVN offered amnesty to VC defectors.

CHINOOK: the CH-47 cargo helicopter; also called "Sh_ thook" or "Hook."

CHOGIE, CUT A CHOGIE: to move out quickly. Term brought to Vietnam by soldiers who had served in Korea.

CHOI OI: Vietnamese term, exclamation like "Good heavens" or "What the hell!"

CHOKE: peanut butter.

CHOPPER: helicopter.

CHURCH KEY: bottle opener.

CLACKER: firing device ("exploder") for triggering claymore mines and other electrically initiated demolitions.

CLAYMORE: a popular, fan-shaped, antipersonnel land mine.

CO: commanding officer.

CONG BO: water buffalo.

CONG KHI: monkey.

CONG MOUI: mosquito.

CONTACT: condition of being in contact with the enemy, a firefight, also "in the sh_t."

CONUS: Continental United States.

COOK-OFF: a situation where an automatic weapon has fired so many rounds that the heat has built up enough in the weapon to set off the remaining rounds without using the trigger mech. This was common in the 50 cal., and the only way to stop it was to rip the belt.

C's: C-RATIONS, C-RATS, CHARLIE RATS, or COMBAT RATIONS—canned meals used in military operations.

CYA: cover your ass.

CYCLO: a three-wheel passenger vehicle powered by a human on a bicycle.

DEEP SERIOUS/DEEP SH_T: the worst possible position, such as being nearly overrun.

DEROS: date eligible for return from overseas; the date a person's tour in Vietnam was estimated to end.

DET CORD: detonating cord. An "instantaneous fuse" in the form of a long thin flexible tube loaded with explosive (PETN). Used to obtain the simultaneous explosion from widely spaced demolitions, such as multiple claymores. Transmitted the explosive chain at 25,000 feet per second. Also used to fell trees by wrapping 3 turns per foot of tree diameter around the tree and firing.

DEUCE: two.

DEUCE-AND-A-HALF: 2.5-ton truck.

DI DI MAU: move quickly. Also shortened to just "Di Di."

DINKY DAU: Vietnamese term for "crazy" or "You're crazy."

DI WEE: captain.

DOC: what the grunts would call medics.

DONUT DOLLY: American Red Cross Volunteer--female. Morale boosters.

DU MI AMI: the F-word with maternal overtones.

DUNG LAI: Vietnamese for "STOP!" or "HALT!"

DUSTOFF: a nickname for a medical evacuation helicopter or mission.

FIELD OF FIRE: area that a weapon or group of weapons can cover effectively with fire from a given position.

FIREFIGHT: exchange of small arms fire between opposing units.

FIRE FOR EFFECT: when all ordnance was aimed at the enemy in continual firing.

FIRE MISSION: an artillery mission.

FIRST SHIRT: 1st Sergeant. (Also called Top).

FNG: most common name for newly arrived person in Vietnam. It was literally translated as a "F--kin' new guy."

FO: Forward Observer, who calls fire missions to artillery and sometimes Air and Naval gunfire.

FRAG: the common term for any grenade.

FREE FIRE ZONE: any area in which permission was not required prior to firing on targets.

FREEDOM BIRD: any aircraft that took you back to the "world" (U.S.A.). It was the aircraft on which you left Vietnam.

FREQ: radio frequency.

FRIENDLIES: U.S. troops, allies, or anyone not on the other side.

FRIENDLY FIRE: "Friendly Fire" was a euphemism used during the war in Vietnam to describe air, artillery, or small-arms fire from American forces mistakenly directed at American positions.

FUBAR: short for "F_ _ked Up Beyond All Repair" or "Recognition." To describe impossible situations, equipment, or persons as in, "It is (or they are) totally Fubar!"

GA MUG: thank you.

G.I.: government issue.

GOOKS: Vietnamese people. Slang expression brought to Vietnam by Korean War Veterans.

GP: general purpose, as in general-purpose tent: large rectangular tent sleeping 10 to 12 men with an aisle down the middle.

GREASE GUN: M2-A1 sub-machinegun, .45cal automatic weapon.

GREEN TRACERS: color left by the ammunition fired from enemy AAA or AK-47s whereby you could track/trace its path.

GREEN-EYE: A starlight scope. A light-amplifying telescope used to see at night.

GRUNT: a popular nickname for an infantryman in Vietnam; supposedly derived from the sound one made from lifting up his rucksack. Also, Ground Pounder.

GSW-TTH: casualty report term meaning "gunshot wound, thru and thru."

GUNG HO: very enthusiastic and committed.

HE: high explosive.

HEAT: High Explosive, Anti Tank.

HEAT TABS: fuel pellets used for heating C-Rations.

HO CHI MINH TRAIL: was a logistical system of roads and trails that ran from the Democratic Republic of Vietnam (North Vietnam) to the Republic of Vietnam (South Vietnam) through the neighboring kingdoms of Laos and Cambodia. The system provided support, in the form of manpower and materiel, to the National Front for the Liberation of South Vietnam (called the Vietcong or "VC" by its opponents) and the People's Army of Vietnam (PAVN), or North Vietnamese Army, during the Vietnam War.

HOOTCH: house or living quarters or a native hut.

HORN: radio, "Get the CO on the horn..."

HOSE (DOWN): massive automatic weapons fire, as from a mini-gun, Spooky or other high firepower gunship. Basecamp perimeters suspected of being infiltrated by sappers would be "hosed down" by gunships and "mad minutes."

HOT: dangerous, such as Hot LZ (where aircraft are receiving enemy fire). Also, see Red.

HOT HOIST: extraction of a soldier by helicopter, using its hoist due to the triple canopy, while under fire.

HOT TOC: haircut.

HQ: headquarters.

HUEY: nickname for the UH-series helicopters: "utility helicopter."

HUMP: to slog around on foot. Grunts in the bush.

ILLUM: illumination. Flares dropped by aircraft and fired from the ground by hand, artillery or mortars.

INCOMING: receiving enemy mortar or rocket fire.

IN COUNTRY: Vietnam.

INSERTION/INSERTED: secret helicopter placement of combat troops in an operational area.

INTEL: intelligence.

KHONG BIET: Vietnamese for "I don't know" or "I don't understand."

KHA: Killed Hostile Action.

KIA: Killed In Action.

KLICK, K: short for kilometer (.62 miles).

KOON SA: the wacky weed, marijuana.

KP: kitchen police.

LAI DAI: "Bring to me" or "Come to me."

LA VAY: beer.

LAW: (Law) M72 Light Antitank Weapon. A shoulder-fired, 66mm rocket with a one-time disposable fiberglass launcher.

LAY CHILLY: lie motionless.

LBJ RANCH: (L-B-J) the Long Binh Stockade. The last word was changed to make a pun on the initials of President Lyndon Baines Johnson.

LEATHERNECK: term for a MARINE.

LIFER: career soldier.

LIGHT UP: to fire on the enemy.

LIMA-LIMA: low level, as in aircraft altitude GCI —Ground-Controlled Intercept.

LOACH OR LOH: light observation helicopter, notably the OH-6A.

LOCK AND LOAD: meaning to chamber a round in your weapon.

LONG GREEN LINE: column of infantry advancing through jungle terrain.

LP: Listening Position. A 2-3-man post placed outside the barbwire surrounding a firebase. Each would lay out claymore mines; they would have 1 radio and take turns during the night listening and looking. They were the early warning for the troops inside the perimeter.

LRP OR LRRP: (Lurp) Long-range Reconnaissance Patrol.

LURPS: Long-range Reconnaissance Patrol members. Also, an experimental lightweight food packet consisting of a dehydrated meal and named after the soldiers it was most often issued to.

LZ: landing zone.

M11: large, anti-malaria pill (Chloroquine). Taken every Monday, produced diarrhea.

M-14: .30 cal, select-fire rifle used in early portion of Vietnam War.

M-16: nicknamed the widow-maker, the standard American rifle used in Vietnam after 1966.

M-60: American-made 7.62mm (.308 cal) machine gun.

M-79: single-barreled, break-action grenade launcher, which fired 40mm projectiles, nicknamed the "Blooper" aka "Thumper" or "Thumpgun."

MAD MINUTE: concentrated fire of all weapons for a brief period of time at maximum rate; also called "Mike-mike."

MAMA-SAN: mature Vietnamese woman.

MASH: Mobile Army Surgical Hospital.

MEDEVAC: medical evacuation by helicopter; also called an "Evac" or "Dustoff."

MIA: Missing In Action.

MIC: microphone.

MIHN OI: sweetheart.

MIKE: minute. Such as, "Move out in two-zero Mikes..." (20 minutes).

MIKE-MIKE: millimeters, as in, "it's a 60 Mike Mike" (60mm mortar).

MILLION DOLLAR WOUND: a wound or injury that got you sent home to the US.

MOS: Military Occupational Specialty--the job designator; one's job title.

MOUA: rain.

MPC: Military Payment Currency; used instead of U.S. dollars.

MULE: small 4-wheeled cargo vehicle.

NAPALM/NAPE: An incendiary used in Vietnam by French and Americans both as defoliant and antipersonnel weapon. Consisted of a flammable organic solvent, usually gasoline gelled by soap. Delivered by bombs or flamethrower, napalm clung to the surfaces it touched, holding the burning solvent in place on the target.

NCO: noncommissioned officer.

NDP: night defensive position.

NEWBIE: any person with less time in Vietnam than the speaker.

NOOK: water.

NOOKDAU: ice.

NO SWEAT: can do...easily done or accomplished.

NON LA: conical hat, part of traditional Vietnamese costume.

NUC or NOUC: water.

NUMBER ONE: good.

NUMBER TEN: bad.

NUMBER TEN-THOUSAND: very bad.

NUOC MAM: fermented fish sauce, called "armpit sauce" by many.

NVA: North Vietnamese Army, or referring to a soldier in the North Vietnamese Army.

OD: olive drab color, standard "Army Green" color; also, Officer of the Day.

ONE DIGIT MIDGET: a soldier with less than ten days left in Vietnam.

ONE O DEUCE: refers to a 105mm howitzer. Many do not know the 105mm is actually 102mm.

OUC-DA-LOI: Vietnamese for Australian.

P-38: can opener for canned C-rations.

PAPA-SAN: an elderly Vietnamese man.

POINT MAN: lead soldier in a unit cutting a path through dense vegetation if needed and constantly exposed to the danger of tripping booby traps or being the first in contact with the enemy.

PONCHO LINER: nylon insert to the military rain poncho, used as a blanket.

POP: generically, to 'trigger' or 'initiate', as in "...pop a flare."

POP SMOKE: to mark a target, team sight (location), or Landing Zone (LZ) with a smoke grenade.

PRC-25: nicknamed Prick. Lightweight infantry field radio.

PRC-77: radio, similar to PRC-25 but incorporated an encryption feature for secure communication.

PROJOS: is a term for a howitzer projectile used by pilots transporting same.

P's: piasters, the Vietnamese monetary unit.

PSP: Perforated Steel Plate. Construction panels, about 3'X8', made of plate steel, punched with 2" holes, and having features on the sides for interlocking together. PSP could be linked together to surface a road, airstrip, etc. or several sheets could be linked into a large plate to form the roof of a bunker, fighting hole, etc., usually covered with sandbags.

PUCKER FACTOR: assessment of the "fear factor," as in the difficulty/risk in an upcoming mission.

PUFF (the Magic Dragon): AC-47 aircraft fitted with side-firing mini-guns and flares.

PUSH: referring to a radio frequency, ie 'PUSH 71.675' meaning a frequency of 71.675 megahertz.

PX: Post Exchange.

QC: Qua^n Ca~nh, which is the Vietnamese equivalent of an American MP.

QUAD 50s: A World War II vintage, anti-aircraft weapon used in Vietnam as an anti-personnel weapon. It consisted of four electric, solenoid-fired, 50 cal. machine guns mounted in a movable turret, sometimes put on the back of a deuce-and-a-half. It was used for firebase and convoy security.

RECON: reconnaissance.

REDLEG: or cannon-cocker: Artilleryman.

RED LZ: landing zone under hostile fire.

REMF: Rear Echelon Mother F_ _ker. Nickname given to men serving in the rear by front-line soldiers.

ROCK 'N' ROLL: to put a M16 rifle on full automatic fire.

ROKs: Republic of Korea ground troops.

ROME PLOW: large bulldozer fitted with a large blade, used to clear jungle and undergrowth in order to make friendly operations easier in that area. The name Rome Plow was derived from the city of Rome, GA where the large blades were manufactured.

ROUND EYE: slang term used by American soldiers to describe another American or an individual of European descent.

RPD: enemy weapon: light machine gun.

RPG: Russian-manufactured antitank grenade launcher; also, rocket-propelled grenade.

RPG SCREEN: chain link fence erected around a valuable position to protect it from RPG attack by causing the enemy rocket to explode on the fence and not on the protected bunker, etc.

R & R: rest-and-recreation vacation taken during a one-year duty tour in Vietnam. Out-of-country R & R was at Bangkok, Hawaii, Tokyo, Australia, Hong Kong, Manila, Penang, Taipei, Kuala Lampur or Singapore.

In country R & R: locations were at Vung Tau, Cam Rahn Bay or China Beach.

RTO: Radio Telephone Operator who carried the PRC-25.

RUCK, RUCKSACK: backpack issued to infantry in Vietnam.

RVN: Republic of Vietnam (South Vietnam).

SAME-SAME: same as....

SAPPERS: North Vietnamese Army or Vietcong demolition commandos.

SAR: search and rescue.

SKY PILOT: another name for the Chaplain.

SEA: Southeast Asia.

SEARCH AND CLEAR: offensive military operations to sweep through areas to locate and attack the enemy.

SEARCH AND DESTROY: offensive operations designed to find and destroy enemy forces rather than establish permanent government control; also, called "Zippo missions." In '69, while with the Big Red One, we received a directive that we were no longer allowed to use the term "search and destroy" to refer to our missions. We were told to use the term "reconnaissance-in-force" or RIF. We generally thought of this as chicken sh*t!!

SHACKLE: encrypt, a method of encoding sensitive information, such as unit locations, in order to be able to send the information by radio.

SHAKE 'n BAKE: an officer straight out of OCS (Officer Candidate School) without any combat experience.

SH_T: a catchall multipurpose term, ie, a firefight was "in the sh_t," a bad situation was "deep sh_t," to be well prepared and alert was to have your "sh_t wired tight."

SH_THOOK: slang for a Chinook Helicopter.

SHORT, SHORT-TIME, SHORT-TIMER: individual with little time remaining in Vietnam.

SIN LOI, MINOI: too bad, honey.

SIT-REP: situation report.

SIX: from aviation jargon: "my 6 o'clock"--directly behind me; hence, my back--cover my back or rear of operation. Also was an infantry term for Commanding Officer.

SIX TYPE: a medic; Doc.

SKATE: goof off.

SLACK MAN: second man in a patrol, behind the POINTMAN.

SLICK: helicopter used to lift troops or cargo with only protective armaments systems.

SLOPE: a derogatory term used to refer to any Asian.

SNAFU: Situation Normal All F_ _ked Up.

SOS: "Sh_t On A Shingle," which is creamed meat on toast.

SPOOKY: a name given to fixed wing gunships.

STAND-DOWN: period of rest and refitting in which all operational activity, except for security, is stopped.

STAY BEHIND (LEAVE BEHIND): ambush tactic where a small group is left behind after a unit breaks camp to ambush enemy sweeping through the 'deserted' area.

STARLIGHT: night-vision telescope, used by snipers and basecamp defense troops to see in the dark.

STERILIZED: restore a site to its original condition before moving out of it.

TEE-TEE: Vietnamese term for "A little bit."

THUNDER ROAD: Highway 13, from Saigon to Loc Ninh, known for many mines, ambushes, etc.

THUMPER (THUMPGUN): M-79 grenade launcher.

TIGER BALM: a foul-smelling oil used by many Vietnamese to ward off evil spirits.

TOC: Tactical Operations Center.

TOT: 'Time On Target' was a multi-battery artillery tactic to provide massive destruction instantaneously.

TRIP-WIRE: thin wire used by both sides strung across an area someone may walk through. Usually attached to a mine, flare, or booby trap.

TRIPLE CANOPY: thick jungle, plants growing at 3 levels — ground level, intermediate, and high levels.

TRUNG WEE: sergeant.

TU DAI: a big concern in country was booby traps. The VC used to warn the locals of booby-trapped areas by posting little wooden signs with those words on it just at the edge of the wood line. Ironically, it was pronounced "To Die." The term "Tu Dai Area" was used in sit-reps.

TWO DIGIT MIDGET: Meant less than one hundred days to that freedom bird out of Vietnam.

UA: unauthorized absence (AWOL).

VC, CONG: Vietcong.

VIETCONG: Communist forces fighting the South Vietnamese government.

WAKEY: the last day in country before going home.

WEB GEAR: canvas belt and shoulder straps used for packing equipment and ammunition on infantry operations.

WHITE MICE: South Vietnamese police. The nickname came from their uniform white helmets and gloves.

WHA: Wounded Hostile Action.

WIA: Wounded In Action.

WILLIE PETER/WILLIE PETE/WHISKEY PAPA/W-P: popular nicknames for white phosphorus mortar or artillery rounds or grenades.

XIN LOI or XOINE LOI: pronounced by GIs as "Sin Loy," meaning "too bad," "tough shit," "sorry bout that." The literal translation is "excuse me."

ZIPPO: flamethrower. Also refers to the popular cigarette lighter of that brand name. The mechanized units called the M113 Armored Personnel Carrier that was equipped with a flamethrower a "Zippo."

About The Author

Joseph (Joe) Edmon Fair Jr. was born on September 4, 1950 in Greenwood, Indiana. His parents had moved from a farming area of South Central Kentucky to the Indianapolis area, looking for work. At nine months old, Fair and his family moved to Louisville, KY. Joe attended Brandeis Elementary School and Parkland Junior High School.

At age 12, they moved back to Adair County, KY where his father once again farmed. He graduated from Adair County High School in May 1968, and entered the US Army in September 1968. Joe served a tour of duty in Vietnam from April 1969 to March 1970, and returned to the US at Fort Meade, Maryland. He married Regnia Gabehart on July 18, 1970. He left the US Army in June 1971.

He joined the Ingersoll Rand Company in September 1971, and remained with the company until May 2011. During his last 16 years, he was the Human Resources Manager.

Joe had two careers going simultaneously as he joined the Kentucky Army National Guard (Bravo Battery, 1st Battalion, 623rd Field Artillery) in October 1974 and remained with the guard until he retired as a First Sergeant E-8 in May 1997. He served in Desert Shield and Desert Storm during the Gulf War, from December 1990 to April 1991 with the guard unit.

Joe and Regnia have three children and seven grandchildren. His retirement is spent enjoying his family (chasing grandchildren), researching and writing about his time in Vietnam, contacting fellow Vietnam soldiers and staying in contact with soldiers he served with in the Kentucky Army National Guard. He also enjoys playing rhythm guitar and singing in a music group called "Ruff-Cut."